TAROT
and the
CHAKRAS

Opening New Dimensions to Healers

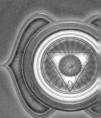

Miriam Jacobs

Schiffer Publishing Ltd®

4880 Lower Valley Road • Atglen, PA 19310

Library of Congress Control Number: 2014931805

Type set in Americana/Mrs Blackfort/Zurich BT

ISBN: 978-0-7643-4663-7
Printed in China

Schiffer Books are available at special discounts for bulk purchases for sales promotions or premiums. Special editions, including personalized covers, corporate imprints, and excerpts can be created in large quantities for special needs. For more information contact the publisher:

Published by Schiffer Publishing, Ltd.
4880 Lower Valley Road
Atglen, PA 19310
Phone: (610) 593-1777; Fax: (610) 593-2002
E-mail: Info@schifferbooks.com

For the largest selection of fine reference books on this and related subjects, please visit our website at www.schifferbooks.com.

We are always looking for people to write books on new and related subjects. If you have an idea for a book, please contact us at proposals@schifferbooks.com.

This book may be purchased from the publisher.
Please try your bookstore first.
You may write for a free catalog.

Images:

Pages 14, 16, 17 and 21 Images adapted by David W Hodges, *Courtesy of Jan W. Cendese, LCSW, LMT, APP*

Page 181- Foot Reflexology Chart, *Courtesy of John Beaulieu*

ancient-tibetan-tangka-White-T-36338719 © Zzvet. Courtesy of www.bigstockphoto.com

"Standing man" © AnnaRassadnikova. Courtesy of www.bigstockphoto.com

"The Seven Main Chakras" © goku347. Courtesy of www.bigstockphoto.com

DEDICATION

Dedicated to Dr. Randolph Stone, DC, DO. NDE

And to my parents Naomi and Howard Jacobs

ACKNOWLEDGMENTS

I'd like to acknowledge and thank the following:

Judy Jacobs and David Harri,s for helping me organize my thoughts and getting me started.

Yvonne Owens provided understanding of my creative process and helped me transcribe much of the written material.

Stephanie Swafford added patience and a fine eye to help with the final edits.

I'd like to especially thank Michael, Denise Holland, Jenny Holland, and Valerie Sonnenthal for encouraging and supporting me through this project.

Thanks also goes out to Caroline Shola-Arewa, John Beaulieu, Linda Berry, Renee Bornstein, Jan Cendese, Darci D'Anna, Celine Germain, Evangel King, George Lakis, Mark Levy, Marty, Hedy Milicevic, Kevan Miller, Jan Milthaler, Daniel Morel, Maureen Parkhurst, Debra Riordan, and Karen Wilson for contributing in their own unique ways.

Gratitude goes to my editor at Schiffer, Dinah Roseberry for believing in this project from the beginning.

CONTENTS

HOME REMEDIES FOR CHAKRA BALANCING

Chapter 13

ZODIAC - ANATOMY
CARD # - SUIT
QUALITY - ELEMENT

Aries forehead
2,3,4 of wands
cardinal fire

Taurus neck
5,6,7 of pentacles
fixed earth

Gemini shoulders
8,9,10 of swords
mutable air

Cancer chest
2,3,4 of cups
cardinal water

Leo solar plexus
5,6,7 of wands
fixed fire

Virgo colon
8,9,10 of pentacles
mutable earth

Libra kidneys
2,3,4 of swords
cardinal air

Scorpio genitals
5,6,7 of cups
fixed water

Sagittarius thighs
8,9,10 of wands
mutable fire

Capricorn knees
2,3,4 of pentacles
cardinal earth

Aquarius ankles
5,6,7 of swords
fixed air

Pisces feet
8,9,10 of cups
mutable water

Crown Chakra
Major Arcana VIII-XIV
PURPLE

Third Eye Chakra
Major Arcana XV-XXI
INDIGO

Ether Chakra
Major Arcana I-VII
BLUE

Air Chakra
Swords
GREEN

Fire Chakra
Wands
YELLOW

Water Chakra
Cups
ORANGE

Earth Chakra
Pentacles
RED

Yvonne Owens

B.A., M.A., Marie Curie Ph.D. Fellow

This is a very different kind of Tarot book,
one that takes the Whole into account.

Miriam Jacobs has crafted an intricate collage of several venerable, spiritual traditions in this book. In the work that follows, the philosophy, science, practice and art of a powerful, new, oracular methodology is unfolded. This combined methodology facilitates a comprehensive range of healing and self-realization. The innovative, interdisciplinary approach revealed in *Tarot and the Chakras* enables readings of a uniquely spiritual, magical, diagnostic, and oracular nature – seldom before synthesized in a single, all-encompassing, healing modality.

Ms. Jacobs bases her approach upon a unique synthesis of ancient and modern methods of "reading" the human, bio-energetic system. Known to Vedic or Ayurvedic traditions as the "Chakra System," to Chinese Medicine as the "Chi," and to world shamanic traditions as the sacred Tree of Life, this wise and elegant bodily consciousness (that we are all hard-wired with at birth) communicates eloquently when approached via Jacobs's methods. Techniques enabling one to perform readings for self and others are revealed through the combined paradigms of astrology, numerology, Polarity Therapy, gemology, and nutrition.

At the root, Ms. Jacobs directs her wisdom teachings to, and through, the body. The tools entailed in this volume are aimed at bringing our experience of ourselves as physical beings into heightened consciousness. As we apply the multifaceted approaches outlined in *Tarot and the Chakras,* we come into an expanded awareness of ourselves as spirit in matter, and of matter AS Spirit. We understand the physical world, and ourselves as vital components within it, as inspirited and inspired by the Divine. For Matter (Mater Materia) is Energy, which is Consciousness, which is Spirit – as Miriam Jacobs demonstrates so ably and well. This book cannot fail to empower all who read it.

INTRODUCTION

This book brings together the ancient
systems of *Tarot and the Chakras*.

My experiences of being an artist, a healer, and Tarot card reader have inspired me to make this connection through energy and the elements. Connecting the Tarot to the Chakras strengthens and deepens both systems, making the two more accessible for new explorers and widening the scope of observation for others.

My own healing process through the years, especially overcoming a Near Death Experience (NDE) at three years old, gave me an opportunity to look at things differently. The experience was a gift that changed me. For many years, my thoughts and experiences seemed unusual, like a huge obstacle. This led me on a quest for health and self-discovery. It is through my desire to articulate what I intuitively know and have read that I write this book: that all things are connected. We live in a world of names and form. Obtaining the essence is the most important aspect of life, in my estimation, though following what feels right still needs a structure.

Nowadays, almost dying, or dying and coming back to life, is termed a Near Death Experience (NDE), as discussed by Raymond Moody. People with NDEs report having similar experiences. They see their lives flash by before them, see a tunnel of light, and often meet deceased relatives. Someone (an angel or a guide) tells them they must go back to their living world. None of these experiences are exactly the same. Some people have harrowing experiences. Most find a sense of wellbeing, and afterwards, they have a new sense of purpose. Many NDE-ers report an increase of healing abilities and psychic phenomena. Most help their friends and family to overcome a fear of death.[1]

I discovered the connection between Tarot and the Chakras by examining charts. The charts helped me to remember and organize material so I could utilize the information. I started to compare and contrast charts of Tarot, Chakras, and the Elements found in Polarity Therapy. Colors matched up with Elements and Elements matched up with the Tarot suits, and they all

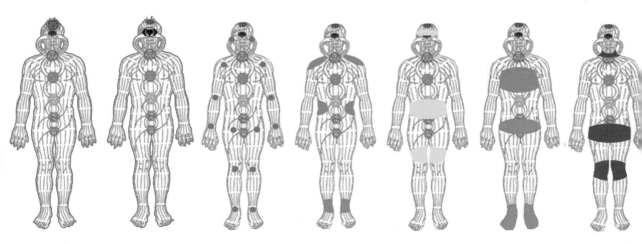

matched up to the Chakras. Eventually, I began creating my own charts. Tarot and Chakras are clearly bridged by the Elements. Astrology and Ayurveda fit in there as well.

ELEMENT	CHAKRA	TAROT SUIT
Ether	Throat, Third Eye, and Crown (higher realms)	Major Arcana
Air	Heart	Swords
Fire	Solar Plexus	Wands
Water	Sexual	Cups
Earth	Root	Pentacles

Tarot helps me to make personal choices and to see the underlying reasons behind events in my life. The readings help focus my intuition and affirm my aim to get to the essence of what I am sensing. Lining up my Chakras in meditation helps me to ground and focus my own energy with efficiency. Incorporating the two systems in my life makes everything seem a lot easier. Tarot gives me meaning and Chakra meditations smooth the edges.

This book is not about precise and specific facts. It is about bridging well-known spiritual systems and practices that have been around for centuries. It is about imagining, sensing, and feeling within a structure – and being creative in finding your own process of healing. It is about you broadening your horizons.

This book offers suggestions for supporting a holistic view of the body, mind, and Spirit. Through Tarot card attributes, advice and stories, and through suggested practices, home remedies, and body practices, we find meaning and ways to balance, connect, and prosper. Everything has a pattern, and once you see those patterns and their underlying systems, everything gets easier. This book offers just that. Let the Tarot help you see those patterns, facilitating your informed and inspired choices and life path directions.

GLOSSARY OF WISDOM SYSTEMS

ASTROLOGY is a tool for understanding the cycles of life based on the positions of the moon, sun, and stars. It shows us how planetary positions affect us when we are born and how those positions influence us daily.

When we understand the collective energies that are happening in the cosmos, we can do two things:

- Work with how the energy is manifesting in our own lives
- Understand and empathize with others' choices, moods, and behaviors

To me, this is the real gift of Astrology. It's not only a model of the world (like science, or religion, or philosophies), but it brings self-knowledge and the connection with others. And that connection can lead to compassion, harmony and love.[1]

Renée Bornstein
Psychological Astrologer and Director of
Café Aquarius Astrology Center, Emeryville, CA[2]

Ayurveda

AYURVEDA is the ancient holistic science of healing from India. It translates as knowing daily life. Ayurvedic belief is that each individual comes into the world with a specific constitution made up of a unique predominate balance of universal elements. Constitutional types are known as doshas. Each dosha has a particular set of qualities that are expressed in the body by physical features, skin and hair qualities, attitudes, and personality types.

THERE ARE THREE MAIN DOSHAS:

VATA
A combination of Ether and Air Elements

PITTA
A combination of Fire and Water Elements

KAPHA
A combination of Water and Earth Elements

WE ARE NEVER JUST ONE DOSHA, WE USUALLY
HAVE A PREDOMINANCE OF ONE OR TWO DOSHAS.
IN TAROT TERMS, DOSHAS COULD TRANSLATE LIKE THIS:

VATA	Ether and Air	Major Arcana and Swords
PITTA	Fire and Water	Wands and Cups
KAPHA	Water and Earth	Cups and Pentacles

To find balance, we are always attempting to get back to the dosha combination we came into this life with, which represents our natural, primary, optimally balanced state. This is achieved mainly through the digestive system through recommended dietary changes. Foods, including herbs and spices, have elemental qualities that affect the doshas. Lifestyle changes, such as exercise, meditations, receiving bodywork, and self-administered cleansing processes may also be included. Only a trained practitioner of Ayurveda or related practices can really make an accurate assessment.

In recent times, the concept of different body types, needing different treatments, has become very popular. Ayurveda practices represent the most comprehensive methods for making these assessments. Polarity Therapy distills Ayurveda teachings into accessible terms, making them easier to understand. This essential distillation of teachings was evident in the methods by which Polarity Therapy developer Dr. Randolph Stone (1890–1981) first introduced Polarity to his students in the States. The influence of dietary changes is seen throughout Stone's work, especially in his Health Building discussions. These distillations can be translated into correspondence aspects of the Tarot and the traditional suits of elements. See the above chart.

Polarity Therapy

POLARITY THERAPY is a profound holistic health care system that balances life energy in the body. It is based on the five universal elements (Ether, Air, Fire, Water, and Earth). Polarity Therapy was developed by Dr. Randolph Stone), a chiropractor, osteopath, and naturopath. Dr. Stone traveled the world to discover different methods of healing and found that energy was the source of healing all disease.

POLARITY THERAPY ADDRESSES FOUR COMPONENTS:

1. **Bodywork** – to evaluate and align the body with Spirit,
2. **Nutrition** – which refers to health building and cleansing diets, and
3. **Exercises** – which consist of yoga-like stretches.
4. **Communications** – a component that increases awareness of the source of tension and fosters positive attitudes. Dr. Stone left this component to be developed by his students.

GLOSSARY OF WISDOM SYSTEMS

Polarity is a practical application of understanding that everything is animated by three energy principles that describe the way energy flows. When they do flow properly, we experience health. These three principles relate to the involution and evolution of energy, or expansion and contraction: Energy starts at a (1) neutral point, (2) expands outward and then (3) contracts inward, going back to the (1) neutral source. Practitioners are trained to track this energy flow and, mainly through types of touch in bodywork, support the client in balancing their energy and regaining health.

Polarity Therapy gives astrological references to anatomy. The Polarity Therapy bodywork protocols (set up for learning purposes, but not necessarily followed, *per se*) and yoga-type exercises reflect this. Polarity Therapy's astrological references partner perfectly with the astrological references of the Tarot. I was amazed to find that the three principle types of touch showed up astrologically in cardinal, fixed, and mutable signs. See chart on page 8.

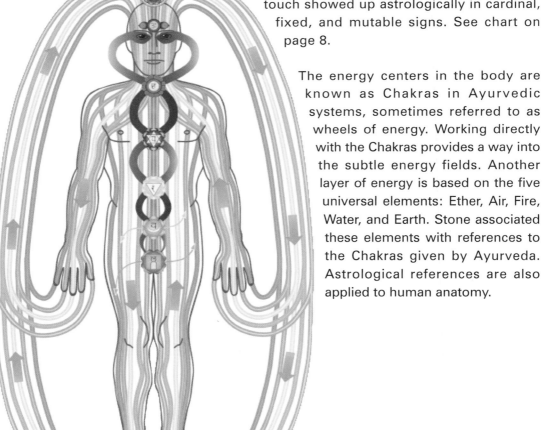

The energy centers in the body are known as Chakras in Ayurvedic systems, sometimes referred to as wheels of energy. Working directly with the Chakras provides a way into the subtle energy fields. Another layer of energy is based on the five universal elements: Ether, Air, Fire, Water, and Earth. Stone associated these elements with references to the Chakras given by Ayurveda. Astrological references are also applied to human anatomy.

Numerology

NUMEROLOGY is the relationship between numbers and physical objects or living things. It interprets the numbers of the spelling of your name and birth date as a divinatory/philosophical system often based on early philosophical theories. Numerology appears in both the Major and Minor Arcana cards.

Kabbalah

KABBALAH is barely mentioned as a connecting system in this text. It can be seen in the foundations of Tarot and occult magic. These versions were most likely crafted in the 15th century. Tarot gives a pictorial and symbolic version of Kabbalah. The Hermitic Order of the Golden Dawn (1890–1920) brought this connection to light. The Golden Dawn initiated its members by using rituals based on the Tree of Life. Members were graded on how far they could go in their mystical path. The Golden Dawn showed the 22 pathways of the Tree of Life as having references to the 22 Hebrew letters and the 22 Major Arcana cards. The connections to be found in the Tree of Life and early, written versions of the Kabbalah system are multi-layered and rich.

Kabbalah is the metaphysical foundation of Jewish Mysticism, also found as an a *priori* concept in Christian and many Eastern religions. It literally means "tradition," or "to receive." During the early years of its practice, after its origins in the 1st century, it was only handed down orally. Written versions began showing up from the 12th century onward that emphasized different aspects of the Kabbalah; some showed clear associations with the Bible, while some versions became more shamanistic and magical.

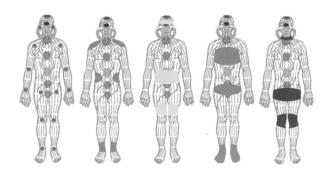

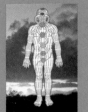

CHAPTER 1

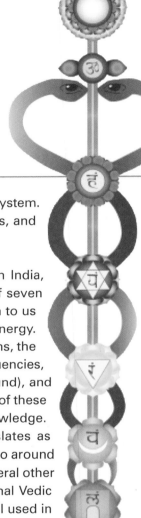

The Chakras

This book integrates Tarot within the framework of the Chakra system. Further, it gives suggested exercise practices, home remedies, and meditations to facilitate the guidelines given by the Tarot.

For centuries, the spiritual systems of ancient civilizations in India, Tibet, and China have all come to a similar understanding of seven basic energy centers that line up along the spine, best known to us as "Chakras." They can be described as swirling vortexes of energy. Chakras are subtle energy centers that regulate bodily functions, the senses and the mind. Each Chakra has specific vibrational frequencies, which are associated with the light spectrum (color), biji (sound), and iconography (symbol) that help in tuning into the Chakras. All of these symbols are derived from ancient Sanskrit systems of knowledge. Sanskrit is the ancient language of India. "Sanskrit" translates as "perfect," "whole," or "pulled together." It can be traced back to around 500 B.C. Languages such as Hindu and Bengali, as well as several other Indian languages, are derived from Sanskrit, and many original Vedic and Hindu texts were written in this ancient language. It is still used in Buddhist chants and Hindu prayers around the world.

CHAKRA	ELEMENT	SUITE	COLOR
Crown	Major Arcana	XV–XXI	Purple
Third Eye	Major Arcana	VIII–XIV	Indigo
Throat	Ether/Major Arcana	I–VII	Blue
Heart	Air	Swords	Green
Solar Plexus	Fire	Wands	Yellow
Sexual	Water	Cups	Orange
Root	Earth	Pentacles	Red

The seven main Chakras connect the microcosm (ourselves) to the macrocosm (the world). They also connect us to our past, present, and future. It is here that Chakras bridge body and consciousness. Each Chakra, with its specific vibratory frequency, corresponds to a different aspect of your life. Each may be focused upon through meditation or visualization to regulate bodily function and peace of mind. The seven Chakras reflect the process of how Energy manifests as matter in the physical body. Energy moves down the spine through each of the Chakras, becoming denser vibratory frequencies as it descends. Working with Chakras is the most direct way to change the subtle energy field and get to the core keys of healing, if you can connect to them. Throughout this book are suggestions for ways to do that.

THE CHAKRA SYSTEM

Crown Chakra
Violet

Brow Chakra
Indigo

Throat Chakra
Blue

Heart Chakra
Green

Solar Plexus Chakra
Yellow

Sacral/Pelvic Chakra
Orange

Root/Base Chakra
Red

The two upper Chakras are the bridge between the universal Spirit and the body. In a sense they rule our Spirit. The lower five Chakras have elemental/suit associations. The fifth Chakra, the Ether or throat Chakra, bridges Spirit to the body. Besides the seven major Chakras, there are twenty-one minor Chakras, forty-nine minute ones, and hundreds of minuscule Chakras. Sometimes they are called nadis (nerves). In Chinese medicine, these are analogous to acupuncture points. In Ayurveda, they are analogous to marma points.

The colors follow the color spectrum, beginning with the delicate frequency/color (or light vibration) of violet at the top of the head, and ending with red at the bottom of the spine. The symbols are used for visualization during meditations. The symbols are sometimes called "lotuses" because, as the subtle nerves, or nadis, converge into the center, they generate the appearance of a lotus. The sounds are pure notes, to be vocalized with long vowels, and meant to vibrate to specific locations in the body, thus moving the energy. If you try this and bring the sound inward,

THE CHAKRAS & THE TAROT

you will notice the vibratory tones move to the correlating Chakra frequency and its physical location in the body.

The Ayurvedic system gives the same elemental names to the five lower Chakras beginning at the throat, and following their way down to the sacrum. The two upper Chakras, the Third Eye and the Crown Chakra, correspond to the individual's connection to Spirit and the Universe. Polarity Therapy systems acknowledge and incorporate this ancient healing wisdom in approaching the entire body/mind/Spirit organism.

Energy is flowing through our bodies at all times, needing to be both open, and to have functioning boundaries at the same time. Maintaining this equilibrium requires intention and some focus. If Chakras are too open, energy will leak. If they are too closed, there is too much contraction, and energy cannot enter the body. Lining up the Chakras, un-blocking and freeing their motion and energy flow enables them to spin appropriately.

This can be achieved through meditation, the use of sounds, visualization, the use of gems and crystals, and by incorporating the messages of the Tarot.

The Tarot

I've chosen to put the Major Arcana cards ascending upwards from the Ether Chakra to the Third Eye and then to the Crown, to make sense of how the Tarot relates to the higher realms of the Chakras.

There are no elements per se for the top two Chakras. Many times these Chakras are given the aspects of sound and light, respectively.

Tarot is a system of divination using a deck of cards. Tarot consists of 78 cards. The origins of the Tarot are unclear. Some believe the Tarot dates back as far as ancient Egypt and relates to the Tree of Life (Kabbalah). Tarot might have originally been a "Book of Wisdom" or a pictorial way for gypsies, who spoke different languages, to communicate. Many believe the first deck was a game made as a wedding gift for the marriage union between the Visconti and Sforza families in 15th century Renaissance Italy.

After the Renaissance, when the Inquisition extended its reach, the Tarot was considered a form of divination, and therefore, along with Astrology, Palm Reading and other oracular practices, was rejected, considered evil, and feared. In the early 20th century, however, occult groups began to form and new interpretations of Tarot decks began to appear. Two different decks that are now the basis for most contemporary Tarot decks were created. Both decks came out of the secret Society of the Golden Dawn in Britain: The *Rider/Waite* deck, (*Rider* being the publisher) was designed in 1910 by Arthur Edward Waite and illustrated by Pamela Coleman Smith. This Tarot deck gave pictorial images for every card. With artist Lady Frieda Harris, Aleister Crowley developed the *Thoth* deck in the 1940s. Crowley added astrological references for every card.

Other important and influential decks are the *Marseille* deck from France and the modern *Visconti Sforza* deck, copied from the famous Renaissance deck. Another branch of Tarot is the modern mystery school version created by Paul Foster Case in 1922, called *The Builders of the Adytum* or *BOTA*. Today, interpretations of the cards vary from reader to reader, and book to book.

THE TAROT IS DIVIDED UP LIKE THIS:

The Major Arcana

TWENTY-TWO MAJOR ARCANA cards narrate the entire range of archetypical experiences. The twenty-two cards also correspond to the twenty-two Hebrew letters and pathways of the Kabbalah (Tree of Life). The Major Arcana cards are the most important part of a reading. These are influences you cannot change, although being made aware of them leads to tremendous insight. The Major Arcana are internal and spiritual in essence.

These cards are your karmic lessons and so have the greatest personal significance in a reading. The Major Arcana bring to our awareness archetypal or universal influences that we are currently experiencing, or soon will. When we recognize patterns that every human shares, we gain understanding and connectedness. The Major Arcana cards are sometimes thought of as secret ways to establish a relationship with the Divine.

Major Arcana cards are more easily comprehended if broken up into sub categories. The Fool card stands alone, in a category of its own, representing everything or nothing.

In the first row are the Ether Chakra cards, I through XII Major Arcana cards. I Magician, II High Priestess, III Empress, IV Emperor, V Hierophant, VI Lovers, VII Chariot all relate to the conscious mind and the body.

In the second row are the Third Eye Chakra cards, XIII through XIV Major Arcana cards. XV Devil, XVI Tower, XVII Star, XVIII Moon, XIX Sun, XX Judgment, XXI World relate to the unconscious mind or the mind.

THE CHAKRAS & THE TAROT

In the third row are the Third Eye Chakra cards XIII through XIV Major Arcana cards. VIII Strength, IX Hermit, Wheel of Fortune X, Justice XI, Hanged Man XII, Death XIII, Temperance XIV relate to the subconscious mind or the spirit.

Major Arcana cards categorized this way are mentioned in various Tarot texts.[1]

CHAKRA			0	FOOL			
Ether	I Magician	II High Priestess	III Empress	IV Emperor	V Hiero-phant	VI Lovers	VII Chariot
Third Eye	VIII Strength	IX Hermit	X Fortune	XI Justice	X11 Hanged Man	XIII Death	XIV Temper-ance
Crown	XV Devil	XVI Tower	XVII Star	XVIII Moon	XIX Sun	XX Judgment	XI World

The Minor Arcana

Forty Minor Arcana cards describe the matter at hand with the help of numerology and elemental energies. The Minor Arcana are similar to a deck of playing cards:

Air/Swords being spades
Fire/Wands being clubs
Water/Cups being hearts
Earth/Pentacle being diamonds

The Minor Arcana cards describe the details. They represent more diffuse energy than the Major Arcana. The Minors describe the possibilities of how things are or may play out in the real world. They conform to the physical world.

ELEMENTAL QUALITIES OF THE MINOR ARCANA

Air/Swords	Thoughts	Relates to the Heart Chakra
Fire/Wands	Insights	Relates to the Solar Plexus
Water/Cups	Emotions	Relates to the Sexual Chakra
Earth/Pentacle	Physical	Relates to the Root Chakra

The Minor Arcana card suits are associated with the Elements and the Chakras. Each Ace represents the pure essence of that suit/element/Chakra. The numbered cards two through ten have astrological references that correlate with the esoteric anatomy of Polarity Therapy. In this correlation the astrology associations start with Aries at the forehead and end with Pisces at the feet.

ASTROLOGICAL ZONES OF THE BODY

Aries – forehead
Taurus – neck
Gemini – shoulders
Cancer – chest
Leo – solar plexus
Virgo – colon
Libra – kidneys
Scorpio – genitals
Sagittarius – thighs
Capricorn – knees
Aquarius – ankles
Pisces – feet

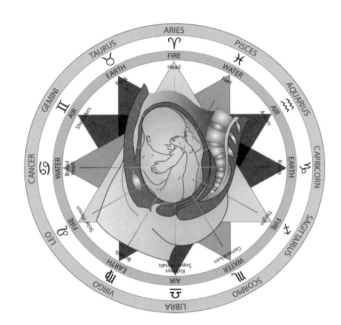

THE COURT CARDS

Associated with the suits are the sixteen Court Cards, which represent specific people or aspects of yourself that influence the matter. The court cards represent psychological states. There are four Courts for each suit. They can be broken up as shown below.

King	Father/wise one
Queen	Mother/nurturer
Knight	Son/young adult
Page	Daughter/child

THE CHAKRAS & THE TAROT

The Court Cards represent all three anatomical references for each suit. They can also cross over to the Element and Chakra relating to that suit.

SUB-ELEMENTS OF THE COURT CARDS

King	Air
Queen	Water
Knight	Fire
Page	Earth

My Interpretation for the Cards

Attributes
The basic meaning of the cards.

Advice
I give simple suggestions to overcome or support challenges presented by that card.

Stories
We remember stories more than facts and meanings. Here, I give examples from stories in my own life, my friends and clients lives, as well as in history, mythology, and popular fiction.

Element Symbols

THE CHAKRAS

 Crown – MA XV–XXI – purple

 Third Eye – MA VIII–XIV – indigo

 Ether – MA I–VII – blue

 Air – Swords – green

 Fire – Wands – yellow

 Water – Cups – orange

 Earth – Pentacles – red

Astrology Symbols

 Aries – Wands – yellow

 Taurus – Pentacles – red

 Gemini – Swords – green

 Cancer – Cups – orange

 Leo – Wands – yellow

 Virgo – Pentacles – red

 Libra – Swords – green

 Scorpio – Cups – orange

 Sagittarius – Wands – yellow

 Capricorn – Pentacles – red

 Aquarius – Swords – green

Pisces – Cups – orange

THE CHAKRAS & THE TAROT

Planet Symbols

Sun – Fire – yellow

Moon – Water – orange

Venus – Earth – red

Mars – Fire – yellow

Mercury – Air – green

Saturn – Fire – yellow

Jupiter – Earth – red

Neptune – Water – orange

Uranus – Water – orange

Pluto – Air – green

Touch Symbols

Rocking	Cardinal
Light or off the body	Fixed
Deep and dispersing	Mutable

Challenge Cards

The 78 tarot cards have only thirteen "challenge cards." These are cards that pose challenging situations or events and difficult emotional states or mental conditions. The energies of these cards challenge you to transform an inner or outer state to resolve the difficult situation they communicate. Of those thirteen cards, six appear in the Air Suit of the Minor Arcana. Since the Air Suit represents thoughts and communication, they are "light" and readily adaptable to transformation and change.

The thirteen challenge cards, as pointed out by Amyeles Arrien in The Tarot Handbook[1]:

3, 5, 7, 8, 9, 10 of Air/Swords
5, 7, 8 of Water/Cups
5, 10 of Fire/Wands
5, 7 of Pentacles

The power of positive thinking has its merits, but how can thinking only be positive? It is better to realize that no situation, no matter how difficult or complicated, lasts forever. And it's very important to realize that any charged emotion associated with difficulties, past or present, can be released. Negative thoughts tend to accumulate and stagnate the flow of air. It's like a stuffy room or strong winds. They can affect our emotions, and our physical body as well. In order to change negative thoughts, it is important to be aware of what the thoughts are connected to and find a way to accept them before attempting to do anything about it. There is great value in differentiating among your thoughts, emotions, and physical sensations. This is best done by simply being present, rather than by judging or over-thinking. In energetic terms, that suggests a state of stillness and peaceful acceptance. After acceptance, change can happen. The charge of counterproductive thoughts, feelings, or physical sensations can be released, transformed, and healed.

Part of my spiritual training as a healer emphasized how "negative" thoughts are our teachers, and are not to be evaded, intensely focused upon, or rejected. Obsessing on or pushing away negative thoughts will only make one's situation worse, and the current state of fear, discouragement, or disappointment harder to overcome. If one stays present and breathes into painful thoughts, simply observing them without judgment, it creates some space around them. One can then afford to feel the feelings associated with the thoughts, which facilitates moving through and beyond them. This practice of mindfulness also develops more compassion for yourself and others.

It has been my experience that meditation also helps you to let go of negative thoughts and the feelings associated with them. It softens your reaction and diffuses resistance. It is resistance that causes psychic, mental, or emotional pain, and can manifest as illness if not released.

CHAPTER 2

Energy

Bibles begin the narrative of their creation with something similar to, "In the beginning there was the word…"[1] Shamanic cultures have long recognized that charged words of intent, or "Words of Power," are magical and potently creative, and that reality – and the world itself – emanates from consciousness (or "Energy") manifested as "shapes of thought," whether written or sounded.

The spoken word is perhaps most potent when it conveys Spirit and intent into physically measurable manifestations as sound vibrations, or wave forms. Everything begins from an energetic wave form. Albert Einstein[2] established in his Theory of Relativity ($E=mc^2$ where E = energy, m = mass and c = speed of light) that everything is actually energy – consistent with a frequency of vibration – and, therefore, Energy equals Matter. He revolutionized the belief that the human body, like all physical structures, is essentially crystallized (or dense) Energy.

There is not one specific source in forming my ways to work with Chakras and Tarot. The yogic traditions of India, and also Ayurveda, assigned Elemental references to the five lower Chakras, and I will often refer to these ancient systems within this book. Behind the crystallization of Energy in the human body are unseen vibrations with positive and negative pulses. A sound is what causes the first vibration of energy from a core source. This energy moves from the core source (Spirit) outward, slowing down and creating matter or physical form. The energy then wants to travel inward, spiraling back to the source to complete the circuit. This is known as expression. In India, this core Energy is known as Prana. In China it is called Chi.

Improper energy flow causes symptoms and disease. This is not electrical energy, although electricity also needs positive and negative pulses to work.

As the energy travels out from the source and gets denser, Ayurveda explains the changes through five universal Elements – Ether, Air, Fire, Water, and Earth. Ether, barely detectable physically, is the lightest, and Earth, as the densest, is the most solid. These Elements are not the elements from your periodic table in high school science class. The 108 elements are shown on the periodic table in order of chemical complexity and periodic properties. The periodic table is a source of key information for scientific research.

ENERGY, ELEMENTS, ASTROLOGY, ETC.

Ether is the name of the "neutral" source in Elemental language. The other four Elements, Air, Fire, Water, and Earth come out of Ether and evolve into substantial matter (the human body, etc.). Elements are essential for functioning on all levels – thoughts, emotions, and our physical bodies.

The Elements of Air, Fire, Water, and Earth are referred to as Active Elements. They are tangible. Correlations to the Active Elements are found in nature.

THE FOUR SEASONS:

Spring	Air
Summer	Fire
Autumn	Water
Winter	Air

THE FOUR DIRECTIONS:

East	Air
South	Fire
West	Water
North	Air

THE ARCHANGELS HAVE BEEN CORRELATED WITH THE ELEMENTS THUS:

Gabriel	Air
Rafael	Fire
Michael	Water
Uriel	Air

In metaphysical wisdom systems, Elements appear in Astrology, Ayurveda, Chakras, Polarity Therapy, Tarot, and more. Some systems refer to the five Elements, and some to four.

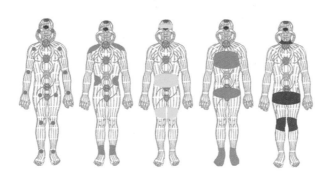

BASIC QUALITIES OF THE FIVE ELEMENTS IN PURE FORM

 The Ether Element

Astrological reflex areas:
The entire wheel of the zodiac

Color: blue
Art: music
Chakra: throat
Sound: Ham
Gemstone: moonstone

What is Ether then? This is not the sub-category of halogenated ether in Organic Chemistry. In metaphysical wisdom systems, Ether is most often equated with space itself. The Ether Element is unique in that it is not associated with one particular zodiac sign. It is associated with the entire wheel of the zodiac, and all elements are expressed through this realm.

Qualities associated with the Ether Element are silence, space, and openness. Ether is the container of all elements, meaning it is the starting point for the four other elements and the space from which they emanate. Ether is the silence through which we are able to hear inner guidance. This is the place between sounds.

ENERGY, ELEMENTS, ASTROLOGY, ETC.

In nature the Ether Element is experienced as wide open spaces, as on a mountaintop, or in the middle of a body of water, an empty room, cathedral, or a large lobby. In the physical body, the Ether Element represents the throat and the ability to swallow. It is also the joints and the craniosacral system because it is all about space.

The Ether Element manifests through the throat and the metabolism of the thyroid gland. This Element is the beginning of the manifestation of the physical body, a sound vibration that relates to the sense of hearing and music. When touching the body, the Ether Element energy will feel like an elongation in the tissue.

Emotionally, we find profound cosmic joy and self-expression with the Ether Element. It gives the ability to express all emotions, most specifically grief, and confers the ability to return to Spirit. We can listen and be present with the Ether Element.

The Air Element

Astrological reflex areas:

Gemini:	shoulders
Libra:	kidneys
Aquarius:	ankles

Color: green
Art: dance
Chakra: heart
Sound: Yam
Gemstone: emerald

The Air Element is the lightest of the Four Active Elements. It is linked to movement, quickness, and agility. It is quick versus stagnant. The Air Element rules our thoughts. The Air Element relates to the wind, from gentle breezes to tornadoes, to sandstorms and gusts. It is associated with anything that flies, from birds to butterflies, and thrown confetti.

Being able to breathe into our lungs and chest is a gift of Air. Air is any kind of mental activity; one can be jittery or high-strung, or have burnt-out nerves. The Air Element is about the sense of touch (the skin) and the three nervous systems: sympathetic, parasympathetic, and autonomic.

The Air Element is heard as a fast, jumpy voice, but it also imbues the quality of dance. Emotionally, the Air Element signifies desire, bargaining, judging, unconditional love, and compassion. It is giddy and joyful.

Mentally, the Air Element likes to analyze and be quick-witted. It is related to getting lost in thoughts or being scattered. At times, a predominance of the Air Element disconnects our emotions from our body. Having lots of ideas can manifest as the inability to choose or as being self-directed and focused. If one's Air Element is stagnant, thoughts can get stuck. Laughter is a great way to move stagnant air.

Air is lighter than all the other elements – so subtle, yet so vital. We can survive for weeks with no food (earth), days with no water, hours without heat, but only minutes without air. Breath is life.

Caroline Shola Arewa
Opening to Spirit.
(London, UK: HarperCollins, 1998), pg.197.[3]

The Fire Element

Astrological Reflex areas:

Aries: forehead
Leo: solar plexus
Sagittarius: thighs

Color: yellow
Art: visual
Chakra: solar plexus
Sound: Ram
Gemstone: coral

Fire is the sun, the energy that sustains everything living. The basic qualities of the Fire Element are obviously heat, brightness, and clarity. Since Fire wants to take charge and insists on being seen, Fire is compelling.

ENERGY, ELEMENTS, ASTROLOGY, ETC.

Even though Fire has many powerful attributes, it can also be very destructive. In nature, any source of heat or combustion belongs to this element. Fire is easily recognized by its flame, found in a warm fireplace, an intense raging forest fire, or a slow-burning candle alike. Fire Element is seen as any type of explosion and eruption, including volcanoes.

In the physical body, the Fire Element governs our upper digestive system, which is our body's way of burning fuel for energy. When Fire is in the tissues, it will feel like shaking. This is a different feeling than the tissue movement of Air. Fire is seen as fevers, all types of inflammation or skin rashes. It is interesting to me that Fire is also the sense of sight and foresight. Viewing the Tarot's association of Fire to Wands helped me to see how this connection was made.

You know a fiery voice when you hear it because it is loud and sharp, sometimes overbearing. Since Fire stands out, it is easy to see how fiery emotions are enthusiastic and excited. Fire insists on power, motivation, and drive. Fire is what causes us to be assertive, boisterous, and maintain high self-esteem. When out of control, Fire is angry and resentful.

Mentally, Fire is direct, blunt, honest, and forthright. Fire takes charge and is forceful.

The Water Element

Astrological reflex areas:

Cancer:	breast
Scorpio:	pelvis
Pisces:	feet

Color: orange
Art: cooking
Chakra: sacral/ sexual
Sound: Vam
Gemstone: pearl

The Water Element conveys our ability to be receptive, to flow, and be flexible. Water is nurturing and facilitates making connections. It is about cyclical energies. Water receives and accepts all things. It also can be overwhelming and/or dissolve boundaries.

In nature, Water is found in the oceans, lakes, rivers, brooks, and streams. It is also seen in gentle rains and hurricanes. Water is the elemental character of all forms of liquid. In the physical body, Water is associated with our breasts and chest, the pelvic region, the feet, lymphatic system, and any kind of secretion glands. Since Water is associated with nurturing and the sense of taste, the artistic attribution is cooking – or nurturing through foods.

The voice quality of the Water Element is flowing and smooth. Emotions in the Water Element are specifically associated with sadness, attachment, holding on, letting go, and going with the flow. Belonging, accepting, and making emotional connections with others is predominant. Water imbalances can entail compulsiveness and addictions.

Depression, thought to be an emotion, is really the inability to express emotions. It is not an emotion in and of itself, but is more about shutting down the emotional realm, and eventually the mental and physical body. Deep depression can sadly lead to far worse issues.

Since Water is all about making connections, on the mental plane its influence will be inclusive or separating. Water understands deep feelings and even has an affinity with the occult. Relationships (more specifically, sexual relationships) are important to the Water connection. Water can cause a lack of boundaries if imbalanced, or a stream that connects everything together if balanced. Water Element is sometimes associated with a "foggy" brain.

Water connects the mother to the child, adults to their sexuality, and our feet to the earth. Our bodies are made up of about 66% water. The earth is about 60% water.

The Earth Element

Astrological reflex areas:

Taurus: neck
Virgo: colon
Capricorn: knees

Color: red
Art: sculpture and aromatherapy
Chakra: root
Sound: Lam
Gemstone: ruby

Earth is energy manifested into form, and defines boundaries. Earth Element is slow and patient. Earth is also solid, secure, and grounded. Earth is practical and wants to complete.

ENERGY, ELEMENTS, ASTROLOGY, ETC.

This element defines our boundaries. Earth is about bringing things into form and actualizing them. It is concerned with survival on this plane, and the structure of our lives in modern times. It relates to material concerns as well as financial security.

In nature, the Element of Earth is all concrete things. It appears everywhere from mountains and deserts to caves and rocks. The Earth Element also is seen in our household structures and walls.

In the physical body, the Earth Element is what gives us structure. It relates to our muscles and bones. In the tissue sense, there is an awareness of the strength and contractedness of muscle tone. Emotionally, the Earth Element gives strength, courage and steadiness. On the flip side, this element can be stubborn and lazy.

Sculpture has been given as the art of the Earth Element. It is three-dimensional and structured. In addition, Earth Element art is also aromatherapy. Earth puts us in touch with the sense of smell.

People who have Earth Element energy are slower than Air or Ether types. The voice of Earth is a low, deep, steady tone. Mentally, Earth wants to organize, be structured, and can become very detail oriented. The Earth Element moves slowly and can be either patient or stubborn.

The Four Active Element Correlations

The Four Active Elements and their correlating seasons each have three astrological signs, one in the beginning of a season, one in the middle, and one at the end of a season. In bodywork, anatomical references are used to balance that Elemental quality of Energy in the body through physical contact of a trained practitioner.

In Astrology these influences are known as cardinal, fixed, and mutable:

CARDINAL SIGNS INITIATE.
They begin ventures, and are inventive and enterprising.
Beginning of a season – rules creativity and action (+)

FIXED SIGNS ARE STEADY.
They solidify ideas.
Middle of a season – maintains and stabilizes (o)

MUTABLE SIGNS PREPARE FOR A TRANSITION.
They are flexible.
Ending of a season – flexible and adaptable (-)

MINOR ARCANA	SEASONAL ASPECT	QUALITY	TYPE OF TOUCH	SANSKRIT NAME
All 2, 3 and 4's	Beginning	Cardinal	Rocking	Rajas
All 5, 6 and 7's	Middle	Fixed	Light	Satvas
All 8, 9 and 10's	End	Mutable	Deep	Tamas

Types of Touch for Tarot/Chakra Therapy

The three gunas (Sanskrit) are a term used in Ayurveda to describe the qualities born in nature. They are the relationship between the expansion, contraction, and neutral quality of energy. Dr. Randolph Stone, creator of Polarity Therapy related the three Gunas to types of touch and a tactile way to get energy to flow through the body.

Rajas is rocking touch (+), Tamas is a deep and dispersing touch (-) and Satvas, a light or off-the-body type of touch (o).

When I incorporated Dr. Stone's chart into the Astrological attributions given to the Minor Arcana, I was thrilled to find that in the Minor Arcana (numbered cards) [see chart at the top of the page].

All 2, 3 and 4's are cardinal signs – a rocking touch (+)

All 5, 6 and 7's are fixed signs – a light or off the body type of touch (o)

All 8, 9 and 10's are mutable signs — a deep dispersing touch (-)

ZODIAC	ANATOMY	CARDS	SUIT QUALITY	ELEMENT
Aries	Forehead	2,3,4 of Wands	Cardinal	Fire
Taurus	Neck	5,6,7 of Pentacles	Fixed	Earth
Gemini	Shoulders	8,9,10 of Swords	Mutable	Air

ENERGY, ELEMENTS, ASTROLOGY, ETC.

ZODIAC	ANATOMY	CARDS	SUIT QUALITY	ELEMENT
Cancer	Chest	2,3,4, of Cups	Cardinal	Water
Leo	Solar plexus	5,6,7 of Wands	Fixed	Fire
Virgo	Colon	8,9,10 of Pentacles	Mutable	Earth
Libra	Kidneys	2,3,4 of Swords	Cardinal	Air
Scorpio	Genitals	5,6,7 of Cups	Fixed	Water
Sagittarius	Thighs	8,9,10 of Wands	Mutable	Fire
Capricorn	Knees	2,3,4 of Pentacles	Cardinal	Earth
Aquarius	Ankles	5,6,7 of Swords	Fixed	Air
Pisces	Feet	8,9,10 of Cups	Mutable	Water

Table of Astrological Natures

♈	ARIES	Cardinal Fire	Focused on new experiences, active and outgoing, assertive, self-willed, starting things off, beginnings	The RAM
♉	TAURUS	Fixed Earth	Secure, stubborn, slow, possessive, strong, loving comfort and beauty, possessions and comforts	The BULL
♊	GEMINI	Mutable Air	Quick, light, talkative, indecisive, adaptable, perceptive and friendly, duality	The TWINS
♋	CANCER	Cardinal Water	Compassionate, sensitive, nurturing, protective, connecting mother – child	The CRAB
♌	LEO	Fixed Fire	Bright, proud, dramatic, adventurous, charging ahead, creative	The LION
♍	VIRGO	Mutable Earth	Meticulous, orderly, service, order and control, detail oriented	The VIRGIN
♎	LIBRA	Cardinal Air	Balanced, just, harmonious balance, and truth	The SCALES
♏	SCORPIO	Fixed Water	Passionate, deep, fearless, Fixed Sign, merging through sexuality, occult	The SCORPION
♐	SAGITTARIUS	Mutable Fire	Big-hearted, idealistic, restless, focused on a target, "out there" energy	The ARCHER
♑	CAPRICORN	Cardinal Earth	Solid, cautious, structured, self-controlled, taking care of earthly needs, career	The GOAT
♒	AQUARIUS	Fixed Air	Trendsetter, extremist, individualistic persons, rulers	The WATER CARRIER
♓	PISCES	Mutable Water	Romantic, idealistic, compassionate, merging with spirituality, letting go of karma	The FISH

Table of Planetary Natures

☉	SUN	Ego-identity, radiant Spirit, individuality
☾	MOON	Emotions, adaptable sense of self, reflective
☿	MERCURY	Reason, skill, intelligence, verbal expression
♂	VENUS	Love, attraction, compassion, connection
♀	MARS	Drive, desire, courage
♃	JUPITER	Truth, faith, grace, optimistic, expansive
♄	SATURN	Order, form, disciplined, fear, contraction, transcendence
♅	URANUS	Free from limitations, willful, inventive, rebellious
♆	NEPTUNE	Formless, escapist, spiritual realized
♇	PLUTO	Transformative, regenerative, subversive

Numbers

1. New beginning, seed, individual
2. Polarity, balance, relationship, opposite
3. Triangle, body/mind/spirit, trinity, synthesis, cooperation, integration
4. Square, four directions/corners/seasons/elements, foundation, stability, order
5. Pentagram, struggle, change, crisis, conflict
6. Cube, triumph, harmony and beauty, reciprocity, exchange, decisive action
7. Chakras/days of the week/wonders of the world, inner work or process, a challenge, mastery
8. Change, inspiration, rhythm or octave, progress
9. Completion, culmination, transition, resolution
10. Manifestation in full form, transformation, abundance[4]

We all want to be happy. Meditation helps give us peace and makes our lives flow with less fear, self-consciousness, and judgment of others.

Meditation empties the mind, whether by a focal point such as a light from candle, a figurine of a deity, or an internal point within the physical body. It is not important whether you follow a guru, meditate in a group or by yourself, listen to a recording, or meditate in complete silence. What matters is that you resonate with the practice and that you keep doing it.
Here is one example of immediate assistance from meditation, involving serious health issues: Gilbert was diagnosed with leukemia. After a successful stem cell transplant, he continued to have ongoing health obstacles, including having to have his gall bladder removed. Gilbert's doctors could not always determine if his body was reacting to the leukemia or to the stem cell transplant. Eventually, Gilbert took matters in his own hands and started meditating. This made such a tremendous difference that his trips to the hospital get less and less frequent. Although Gilbert has not regained complete health, he can handle what comes up in a more equanimous and positive manner.

Many types of focal point mediations visualize aligning the Chakras, starting from a particular Chakra and following through the Chakra sequence, aligning the other Chakras. My practice keeps evolving, but I always seem to come back to energetically and meditatively aligning my Chakras. A Tarot reading is an excellent way to begin.

TAROT SHOWS US WHAT NEEDS FOCUS.
CHAKRAS SHOW US WHERE TO FOCUS.
MEDITATION SHOWS US HOW TO FOCUS.

Always start with an awareness of your breath and notice how it feels to you. Make sure you are comfortable and will not be disturbed. When moving from the Ether Chakra (at the throat) to the Third Eye (center of brow), place the tip of your tongue gently on the roof of your mouth. Go back and forth between two Chakras, blending or melting the colors together. Imagine a swirl of energy spinning around the two Chakras. Do this several times until they feel connected.

Basic Meditation Practice

Start by visualizing either the Crown or the Earth Chakra.

Scan your Chakras individually in succession. Spend about 15–30 seconds at each Chakra.

Take note if there is a particular Chakra that seems stuck or hard to imagine or feel.

Go back to the Chakra that you had trouble with and focus on ways to get it to spin. Try a clockwise and counter clockwise spin. Try sending it light, or pull energy from its neighboring Chakras.

Compassionate Meditation Practice

Breathe in any form of negativity or adversity of yours, or of a person you love, into your heart (Air Chakra). Visualize transforming this negativity into pure white, loving energy and send it out into the world.

Chakras are never closed down completely. They can only slow down. If a particular Chakra is slowed down or hard to connect to, it indicates a blockage in the energy field. Become aware of what this might mean. Look up the designated meanings for this and evaluate whether or not they makes sense. Imagine each Chakra as spinning first counterclockwise, then clockwise.

Look in the "Chakras and the Tarot" chapter to find corresponding Tarot cards. Do any of those cards have advice that rings true for you? Look at the indicated challenges as blocked energy. Challenges are not always associated with only one element.

You may want to get two Chakras to communicate by imagining a cord or color to connect them. The challenge might be a present-day or an old issue that is surfacing.

Ask the cards:

- What are my challenges for this moment, this day, or this week?
- How can I best meet those challenges?
- What Chakra do I need to focus on today?

CHAKRA MEDITATIONS

Crown Chakra Meditation

What is the dialog going on in your head? Where does it come from? How much of it is an illusion? How can you find a quiet clarity? Let the dialogue go and clear the psychic slate. Go to emptiness.

When I visited Tassajara Zen Mountain Center[1], I was struck by the peacefulness. Tassajara is a retreat center in the Carmel Valley of California that offers meditations retreats of the Zen Soto tradition. It is a beautiful environment to meditate, listen to Dharma talks (Zen teachings), hike, and eat healthily.

The Soto Zen meditation allows you to experience a greater openness of being, gained by attaining an awareness of body and breath. Embracing a Zen meditation practice reconnects your heart and mind.

Established by Dogen Zenji in 13th-century Japan, the Soto Zen tradition is now conveyed by Buddhist teachers throughout the world. The belief is that sitting in meditation is itself the realization of Buddha's enlightened nature.

Sit in a lotus position, on the floor with your legs crossed and be very still. If you cannot sit this way, find a comfortable sitting position with your back as straight as possible.

Turn your focus inward and focus on your breath.

Be present with whatever arises.

Third Eye Chakra Meditation

This meditation helps us to focus inward on our inner eye, our internal world, and knowing.

Sit comfortably, preferably on the floor or on a couch in a lotus position.

Place your relaxed hands softly over your closed eyes. Wait until you feel the warmth from your hands soothe your eyes.

Allow your focus to go towards your Third Eye Chakra, the spot on your forehead between your eyes. Get that Third Eye Chakra to spin, deep into your brain and head.

Now, visualize that energy moving up to the top of your head, the Crown Chakra. Connect these two places by imagining a blue to purple cord. Third Eye to Crown, Crown to Third Eye.

Allow the cord to connect in a circular motion. Continue until the right moment, when the energy moves smoothly.

Then place one hand over the throat and the other hand lightly over the heart. Visualize the cord of energy moving to the throat, the Ether Chakra. Imagine the cord changing to a lighter blue color. Now move the energy back up again towards the Third Eye and then Crown.

Push the energy down again, this time moving down towards the heart. Imagine the cord turning green and the Air Chakra.

Next, place one hand over your chest and one near your belly button and pull your energy to this spot. Visualize yellow. This is your Fire Chakra. With fiery energy, follow the cord up the body to the Third Eye and Crown Chakras.

Wait, and then pull the energy back down the body. Place both hands over your lower abdomen, then your groin. Imagine the Water Chakra and the color orange.

Now place your hands on the knees, pressing down slightly. While imagining the cord of energy going to your sacrum and Earth Chakra, visualize it turning red.

After the cord feels solid, visualize it traveling back upward and resting at the Third Eye and Crown. Go back to spinning the blue to purple cords around your Crown and Third Eye.

Slowly open your eyes and come back to the room.

Ether Chakra Meditation

The Ether Chakra is home to your true voice.

Many forms of meditation involve chanting mantras, sacred sounds, or words that bring about a specific transformational vibration. There are most likely hundreds of mantras to chant. Mantras are to be chanted in rapid succession. They are often sung.

CHAKRA MEDITATIONS

In this section, dealing with the "I speak Chakra," I also must mention the power of prayer. Prayer is, in a sense, a form of meditation.

Larry Dossey has written several books on prayer being used for healing. He has documented hundreds of studies that show an organism becomes healthier if a caring loving attitude is directed at it. Dossey goes on to say that it doesn't matter what type of prayer is being used, as the intent behind prayer is love and compassion.

Perhaps a modern version of chanting a mantra would be repeating an affirmation. The difference is that a mantra involves purer sounds, as musical tones, and affirmations are words that tap into our thought process. Words have a tremendous amount of power, so be careful what you ask for. It is also important to go with the feeling. For example: Ryan's car accident was so severe that it left him a quadriplegic. His doctors did not believe that he would ever regain movement of his limbs. Having studied jazz, Ryan was well aware of the healing ability of music. He had his friends and family set up a healing sound environment in his room. To the amazement of everyone, Ryan started to heal. He can now walk and move around. Ryan has dedicated his life to healing others through sound.

Noble Lady Tara, the mother of all Buddhas in Tibet, represents compassion, love, wisdom, and nonviolence. A Tara practice has twenty-one "Praises of Tara," forms of Sanskrit mantras to be chanted while viewing a specific image of Tara. Each praise has a different spiritual attribute to open up very specific channels in the human energy system. It takes a serious commitment to follow through on a Tara practice.[2]

I have simplified this to one specific Tara chant that helped me get through a rough time in my life: *Om Tara Tuttare Ture SoHa*, which translated means "I prostrate to the liberator, Mother of all Victorious Ones." The meaning goes much deeper than that, but this is a great place to start.

When I was exploring a Tara practice, I was interested in what the sound vibration did to my body. It did wonders. Whenever I feel lost, I go back to this chant and ask Noble Lady Tara for help.

Recite the mantra as a continuation in rapid succession, either out loud or to yourself: *Om Tara Tuttare Ture SoHa*. Start off sitting comfortably, preferably with an image of the

Goddess Tara in front of you. Tara images on a tanglin – sacred wall hangings or paper – can be purchased at Tibetan shops, or online. A small statue will do as well. Look at it with softly focused eyes. When this picture becomes more imprinted on your brain, imagine it dissolving into your own being. Saying this particular mantra opens the central channel.[3]

A Tara practice references the subtle energy body, which is very different from the physical body, a clear understanding of which is only gained by serious devotees. In this practice there are three channels: the left, the right, and the central.

> *Begin by saying the mantra, Om Tara Tuttare Ture SoHa.*
>
> *Repeat three times for each of the seven Chakras in succession, beginning at the Crown Chakra.*
>
> *Pause at each Chakra.*
>
> *Focus on how the chant sounds coming from the Ether Chakra.*
>
> *Become aware of how the sound vibrates in the rest of your body.*

Air Chakra Meditation

Focus on the breath. Clear your mind and open your heart. Following the breath is one of the simplest ways to meditate.

> *Sit comfortably. With your right index finger, hold down your left nostril. Breathe in for five counts through the right nostril.*
>
> *Let your abdomen expand with your breath and hold for another five counts.*
>
> *Release the left nostril and breathe out of both nostrils while contracting your abdomen.*
>
> *Repeat seven times.*
>
> *Now, with your right thumb hold your right nostril. Breathe in for five counts through the left nostril.*
>
> *Let your abdomen expand with your breath and hold for another five counts.*
>
> *Release the right nostril and breathe out of both nostrils while contracting your abdomen.*

CHAKRA MEDITATIONS

Variations of this breathing meditation may be done by breathing in one nostril and then out the other, or by rotating sides after one repetition.

Fire Chakra Meditation

I learned early on in my Chakra meditation exploration that my solar plexus, the Fire Chakra, is a perfect place from which to release negative or destructive energy. On the other hand, this is not a good place to take in external energy because it does not filter out incoming, negative energy. I don't think I've ever heard this since, but I still think it is sound advice.[3]

While doing the following meditation, make sure that you get your Fire Chakra to spin. This is where you gain the strength to expel undesirable or "negative" energy. As with the Water and Earth Chakras, let the energy ascend upward through your body and exit from your Fire Chakra. After clearing all the Chakras, end with imagining yourself covered in white, protected light.

Sit comfortably in an undisturbed place.

Place a lit candle in front of you. Make sure the light of the candle is in comfortable view.

With softly focused eyes, gaze at the candle. Empty your mind, line up your Chakras, or make a prayer. What do you see as you gaze into the candle?

Send light from just above your head in through the Crown Chakra.

Breathe in through your nose and spin light energy slowly down the spine one to three times through the Third Eye, Ether, and Air Chakras, as if it were clearing the Chakras.

Now, send that energy out through your solar plexus, allowing negative energy to only pass out of your body. Breathe out through your mouth.

Repeat this for each Chakra.

FIRE CHAKRA TIDBIT

Have you ever felt like someone was consciously or unconsciously trying to throw your ego off balance, or attempting to knock you off your center? If so, here's a practice you can do:

Imagine a mirror around your solar plexus facing outward. This mirror can be a two-dimensional circle or it can be a round sphere that encompasses you. You don't want to throw negative energy or thoughts at someone else because it can come back to you, but what you can do is prevent their negative intentions directed at you, or their conscious or power play, and mirror it back to them.

This is a simple technique I've used with great success. Here's an example of when I worked at a high school.

For several years I worked as the art teacher for a small private high school. It was clear from my first few months that the assistant dean could care less about art education or me. He was not giving me the support a first-year teacher needed, and in my opinion tried to make my job more difficult.

I successfully tried this trick: I visualized a mirror around my Fire Chakra every time I interacted or thought about him. This literally stopped him in his tracks. It was as if he would get distracted and forget about giving me a hard time.

Towards the end of my first year, the assistant dean came up to me and shook my hand. When I asked him what that was for, he said that he wanted to congratulate me on doing such a good job and that being the art teacher in that school was a difficult one. In the years that followed, the assistant dean actually went out of his way to support me.

I suggest you do it every time you are in a Fire Chakra battle, or someone is disturbing your equilibrium and throwing you off balance. Whenever you are in close proximity to that person, or even thinking about them, do not focus negative thoughts on them – just visualize a mirror around your Fire Chakra.

Water Chakra Meditation

The Taoist sage, Mantauk Chia, believes that healing comes from the sexual center of our bodies. He imparts to people how to move and contain this energy. His exercises increase and transform sexual energy (creative energy) into Chi, which is our life force, and then into Spirit energy. He teaches beginning at the lower groin, ascending downward to the perineum and up the spine, stopping at different gates, or stations in the body.

CHAKRA MEDITATIONS

Since Master Chia's exercises focus on beginning at the pelvis, they are easily translated to begin focusing at the Water Chakra. He has inspired this meditation.

Wear loose clothes that do not restrict your waist or lower body.

Sit comfortably on the edge of a chair with your feet flat on the floor.

Breathe in through your nose, slowly expanding the breath into your lower abdomen.

Collect this energy more specifically into your Water Chakra and hold it there for a short while, dropping your focus to your sexual organs. Tighten your pelvic muscles in a holding manner while breathing.

Send this energy further down to your Earth Chakra and the perineum. The perineum is the spot between the sexual organs and the anus.

Explore sending energy back and forth between each of these points. Do not let the energy escape.

Hold the energy, starting with one minute, working up to a few minutes.

Move the energy down to the Earth Chakra and then up the back side of the body to the lower spine, opposite where the Water Chakra is located.

Then move the energy up to the back of the Fire, Air, and Ether Chakras, and then to the Third Eye and the Crown Chakra. Pause and collect the energy in each of these points. (In the Microcosmic orbit system, these points or stations have different names.)

When moving from the Third Eye to the Ether Chakra, place your tongue gently on the roof of your mouth.

Imagine your energy spinning counterclockwise on top of your head.

Now make your journey back down the front of the body, gently pausing at each Chakra, giving it an imaginary spin clockwise.

Rest at the Water Chakra.

Earth Chakra Meditation

A five-pointed star, or pentacle, often appears as the symbol for the Earth Suit of the Minor Arcana of the Tarot, alternating with coins as its symbol and, more recently, crystals. Leonardo da Vinci's "Vitruvian Man" symbol is the image of a human body superimposed upon a pentacle. It shows the "perfect proportions" according to the Renaissance Humanist credo, "Man is the measure of all things," and is based on the correlations of ideal human proportions using geometry described by the ancient Roman architect Vitruvius in Book III of his treatise *De Architectura*.

Sit up tall with your feet on the ground. Imagine the four corners of each foot equally balanced on the ground. Push up or down on any point that does not feel balanced. (If you are lying down, bend your knees so that your feet are flat on the surface, comfortably positioning your "sit bones.")

Feel the bottom of your feet as if they were solidly on the earth, growing roots that are going deep and deeper.

Become aware of energy traveling up your legs, into your ankles, your calves, your knees, and thighs.

Imagine this energy meeting at the base of your spine, the location of your Earth Chakra. Breathe in the color red. Imagine your Earth Chakra spinning clockwise. (Clockwise is however you imagine it.) Simultaneously imagine the roots that you have established coming up from the ground.

Bring the energy from your Earth Chakra up to your Water Chakra. Now see this Chakra spinning, and imagine the color orange.

Bring the energy from your Water Chakra up to your Fire Chakra. Now get that to spin and imagine the color yellow.

Bring the energy from your Fire Chakra up to your Air Chakra. Now get that to spin and imagine the color green.

Bring the energy from your Air Chakra up to your Ether Chakra. Now get that to spin and imagine the color blue.

Bring your energy from the Ether Chakra up to your Third Eye Chakra. Now get that to spin and imagine a deep indigo color.

Bring the energy from your Third Eye Chakra up to your Crown Chakra. Now get that to spin and imagine the color violet.

Reverse and repeat.

What are you feeling in your body? Do you have a sense of being grounded?

CHAKRA MEDITATIONS

Mudras

Mudras are hand positions that aid in our meditation process. They can be used during formal meditations, before going to sleep, while walking, in a meeting, or anytime during the day. The hand positions can be quite simple. They follow the energy lines of the body. Each finger follows a Chakra/Element/Suit line of energy. The mudras help in opening and enhancing the Chakras.

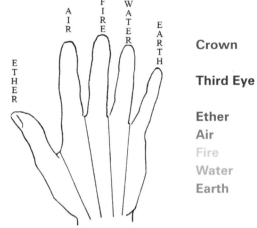

Crown	Hold both hands open and relaxed, facing upward
Third Eye	Hold one hand over the other, with open palms facing up
Ether	Touch both thumbs together
Air	Touch the thumb with the index finger
Fire	Touch the thumb with the middle finger
Water	Touch the thumb with the ring finger
Earth	Touch the thumb with the pinkie

Chakra Statements

Some statements that can be used as affirmations while practicing mudras, either aloud or as silent thoughts are:

"I understand."	**Crown**
"I see."	**Third eye**
"I speak."	**Ether**
"I love."	**Heart**
"I do."	Fire
"I feel."	Water
"I am."	**Earth**

CHAPTER 4

There are symbols that can be cross referenced to correspond to several systems. Noting what these symbols mean is very helpful in understanding the Tarot and its relationship to the Chakras.

About Symbols

At the top of each card description is a series of symbols. They are coded as far as elemental qualities and Chakras. A Sub-Element is determined by another planetary or astrological influence referred to in that particular card.

COLOR SYMBOLOGY

Purple	Crown	MA XV–XXI
Indigo	Third Eye	MA VIII–XIV
Blue	Ether	MA 0–VII
Green	Air	Swords
Yellow	Fire	Wands
Orange	Water	Cups
Red	Earth	Pentacles

MA=Major Arcana

Reading left to right:

Major Arcana: element, Sub-Element, touch, zodiac or planetary influence, Chakra

Minor Arcana: element, touch, planet, zodiac, Chakra

Aces: element, touch, Sub-Element, Chakra

Courts: element, touch, Sub-Element, Chakra

[See charts on pages 23-24.]

USING CHAKRA WORK WITH TAROT

The following charts show the layout of symbols as seen above the individual card descriptions. Aces, Major Arcana, Minor Arcana, and Court cards vary slightly symbol. See individual symbols on pages 23-24.

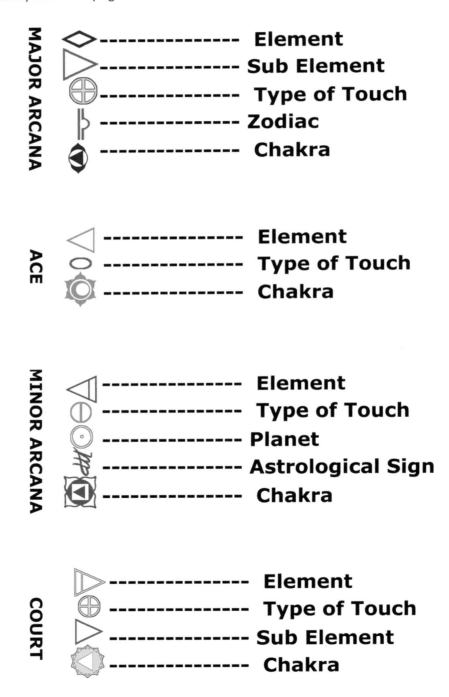

MAJOR ARCANA

- ------------- Element
- ------------- Sub Element
- ------------- Type of Touch
- ------------- Zodiac
- ------------- Chakra

ACE

- ------------- Element
- ------------- Type of Touch
- ------------- Chakra

MINOR ARCANA

- ------------- Element
- ------------- Type of Touch
- ------------- Planet
- ------------- Astrological Sign
- ------------- Chakra

COURT

- ------------- Element
- ------------- Type of Touch
- ------------- Sub Element
- ------------- Chakra

Three Basic Spreads

There are hundreds of Tarot card spreads. Here are three basic ones:

ONE-CARD READING

Pick one card on a particular inquiry as a quick read or a supplement to your activities.

Why try to figure something out when you can ask the Tarot?

While learning the Tarot, it is helpful to pick one card at the beginning of the day and ponder the meaning and references. At the end of the day, look up the meaning. Did it make sense?

FOUR-CARD READING

Focus on your question or intention.

Shuffle the deck and spread out the cards.

Choose four cards, one at a time, and place them from right to left as shown.

You may choose several sets of four for deepening or clarifying your question.

The meaning of a card is strengthened if it is in the placement that corresponds to its element.

For example:

A Fire card in the Fire (first) placement

Weakened cards are as follows:

Water card in a Fire placement
Fire card in a Water placement
Earth card in an Air placement
Air card in an Earth placement

Major Arcana cards always trump a reading. More than one card of the same element or number strengthens the meaning of those cards in the spread.

USING CHAKRA WORK WITH TAROT

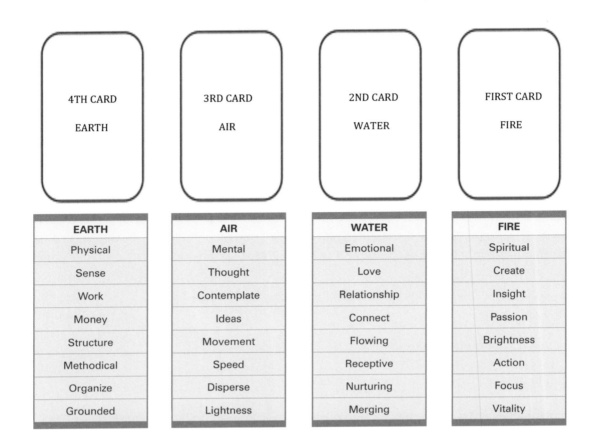

4TH CARD EARTH	3RD CARD AIR	2ND CARD WATER	FIRST CARD FIRE

EARTH	AIR	WATER	FIRE
Physical	Mental	Emotional	Spiritual
Sense	Thought	Love	Create
Work	Contemplate	Relationship	Insight
Money	Ideas	Connect	Passion
Structure	Movement	Flowing	Brightness
Methodical	Speed	Receptive	Action
Organize	Disperse	Nurturing	Focus
Grounded	Lightness	Merging	Vitality

Place and read cards from right to left.

Besides their suit elemental representation, the Court Cards are also represented by sub-elements as shown in the chart at the bottom of page 21.

CHAKRA BODYWORK SPREAD
(TO BE DONE WITH TWO PEOPLE)

Have your client focus on an intention.
Shuffle the deck and spread out the cards.
Have one person choose seven cards, face down.
The other person aligns the cards as they were chosen with the first person's Chakras.
Then read the cards.

Positive/Negative Cards

WHAT DO YOU DO WHEN A CARD IS REVERSED?

Typically, reversals indicate the opposite meaning of a card. When a card is reversed, it is often interpreted as constricted or stagnant energy that needs attention. Please note: The Tarot short list beginning on page 61 includes reversed meanings.

ASTROLOGY, WITH TAROT AND THE BODY

The twelve astrological signs harmonize with twelve designated body points:
They also reflect the 4 key elements (Air, Fire, Water, and Earth). [See chart on page 8.]

Having a basic understanding of astrology and the planets is helpful, although not necessary. Every Minor Arcana card is assigned a zodiac sign and planet. The twenty-two Major Arcana have either a sign or a planet. The Court Cards are represented by elements.

Questions

Instead of asking questions that can be answered with "yes" or "no" responses, consider opened-ended questions.

Recently, I read cards at a high school prom in an affluent community. I only had three to five minutes with each student. Most of them had never had their cards read before prom night. My personal mission was to de-mystify Tarot and lead the students to empower themselves. I told each student as they sat in front of me that I was not going to predict their future. I formalized their question (which also saved time) by having them ask, *How can I best approach my future?*

The answers of support ranged anywhere from how they could approach that night, to college and beyond. One young man affirmed that what really mattered to him was marriage and children. His career was superfluous, to him.

USING CHAKRA WORK WITH TAROT

Suggested questions clients may ask of the cards:

- What can I learn from this situation?
- How can I best approach_____?
- What are the implications of my choice(s)?
- What are and how can I overcome negative circumstances?
- How am I off course?
- What has to happen for me to reconnect to myself/another/a situation?
- What is going on?

How you may guide their inquiry:

- Help set the intention
- Open the conversation
- Lend a witnessing ear
- De-clutter mental and emotional patterns, making the work easier and more effective
- Indicate where in the body to move and balance specific energy
- Support right-thinking by differentiating thoughts, emotions and the physical body
- Strengthen trust in decision making
- Direct where and how the body needs particular attention
- Empower the querent

Basic Bodywork Guide

For somatic bodywork, follow the elemental colors of the chosen Minor Arcana card(s):

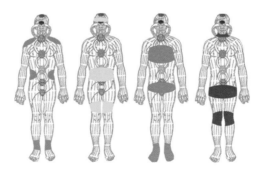

Make two contacts simultaneously, with each hand on a point within the indicated element. (The Aces and the Court Cards point out all 3 anatomical body points of the represented element/suit. For more insights, see various charts throughout this book.)

COLOR	ELEMENT	SUIT
Green	Air	Swords
Yellow	Fire	Wands
Orange	Water	Cups
Red	Earth	Pentacles

Hold the two points and wait for them to come into balance. It will feel like a pulse between the two. Another option would be to contact the various points indicated by the cards in an entire spread. Wait and "listen" for the pulse. Or suggest a meditation, movement, or ritual from your intuition.

Always remember, your presence and intention have an impact that brings conscious awareness. Get creative and record your results.

CHAPTER 5

Author Note:

There will be a more in-depth discussion of these list items in the following chapters.

Elements

THE ETHER ELEMENT

Astrologically reflex areas:
The entire wheel of the zodiac

Color: blue
Art: music
Chakra: throat
Sound: Ham

THE AIR ELEMENT

Astrologically reflex areas:
Gemini • shoulders
Libra • kidneys
Aquarius • ankles

Color: green
Art: dance
Chakra: heart
Sound: Yam

THE FIRE ELEMENT

Astrological reflex areas:
Aries • forehead
Leo • solar plexus
Sagittarius • thighs

Color: yellow
Art: visual
Chakra: solar plexus
Sound: Ram

THE WATER ELEMENT

Astrologically reflex areas:
Cancer • breast
Scorpio • pelvis
Pisces • feet

Color: orange
Art: cooking
Chakra: sacral/sexual
Sound: Vam

THE EARTH ELEMENT

Astrologically reflex areas:
Taurus • neck
Virgo • colon
Capricorn • knees

Color: red
Art: sculpture and aromatherapy
Chakra: root
Sound: Lam

Chakras

CROWN CHAKRA

Location: top of the head
Color: gold, violet, or light
Element: Pure Spirit
Vocalization: silence
Note: B
Symbol: lotus flower with sixteen or a thousand petals
Planet: Sun and Uranus
Sanskrit Name: Shasrara
Meaning: time and space
Main Function: liberating
Quality: fulfillment

THIRD EYE CHAKRA

Location: forehead
Color: indigo
Element: Light
Vocalization: Aum
Note: A
Symbol: eye with two petals
Planet: Jupiter
Sanskrit Name: Ajna
Meaning: perception
Main Function: seat of wisdom
Quality: vision

ETHER (THROAT) CHAKRA

Location: throat
Color: blue
Element: Ether
Vocalization: Ham
Note: G
Symbol: inverted triangle surrounded by a circle
Planet: Mercury
Sanskrit Name: Vishuddha
Meaning: purification
Main Function: communication
Quality: vibration, sound, voice

AIR (HEART) CHAKRA

Location: behind the heart
Color: green
Element: Air
Vocalization: Yam
Note: F
Symbol: six-pointed star
Planet: Venus
Sanskrit Name: Anahata
Meaning: unstuck
Main Function: transformation, holistic
Quality: compassion

FIRE (SOLAR PLEXUS) CHAKRA

Location: base of the sternum, above the navel
Color: yellow
Element: Fire
Vocalization: Ram
Note: E
Symbol: an inverted triangle with ten petals
Planet: Mars
Sanskrit Name: Manipura
Meaning: city of gems
Main Function: supplies energy in the form of heat, power, and enthusiasm; intellectual
Quality: passion and empowerment

SHORT LISTS OF ELEMENTS, CHAKRAS, & TAROT CARDS

WATER (SACRAL/SEXUAL) CHAKRA

Location: lower abdomen
Color: orange
Element: Water
Vocalization: Vam
Note: D
Symbol: moon with six petals
Planet: Moon
Sanskrit Name: Swadistana
Meaning: dwelling place
Main Function: provides sense of self, emotion
Quality: centering

EARTH (ROOT) CHAKRA

Location: base of spine
Color: red
Element: Earth
Vocalization: Lam
Note: C
Symbol: square with four petals
Planet: Earth, and Saturn
Sanskrit Name: Muladhara
Meaning: root/support/foundation
Main Function: embodiment, instinctual
Quality: grounding

Tarot

THE MAJOR ARCANA

0 Fool ....
Qualities: leaping into a new phase of life or spiritual direction, childlike wonder, carefree
Element: Air
Anatomy: ankles
Astrology: Uranus
Reversed: risk averse, over confident
Musings: open to new possibilities, fearless

I Magician ....
Qualities: using all the tools one has, the ability to communicate well, attuned, aware
Element: Air
Anatomy: shoulders
Astrology: Mercury
Reversed: lack of communication, questionable use of will, crossed wires
Musings: ability to make something happen through action, the messenger

II High Priestess ....
Qualities: trusting your intuition and dreams, spiritual mother, psychic ability, follows the natural body rhythms
Element: Water
Anatomy: chest
Astrology: Moon
Reversed: cool, overly introspective
Musings: internal knowing, going on a hunch

III Empress ....
Qualities: nurturing, Earth Mother, grounded energy, fertile and abundant, represents aspects of the female
Element: Earth
Anatomy: neck
Astrology: Venus
Reversed: smothering, clinging attachment
Musings: sees love and beauty in everything

SHORT LISTS OF ELEMENTS, CHAKRAS, & TAROT CARDS

IV Emperor

Qualities: asserting ambitions and confidence, father figure, an established and benevolent leader
Element: Fire
Anatomy: forehead
Astrology: Aries
Reversed: egotistical, self-righteous
Musings: right use of power

V Hierophant

Qualities: teaching in a traditional sense, knowledge and education in an accepted form
Element: Earth
Anatomy: neck
Astrology: Taurus
Reversed: repressive, dictatorial, self-absorbed
Musings: hierarchal structures, practical

VI Lovers

Qualities: duality, partnership, lovers, union, opposites
Element: Air
Anatomy: shoulders
Astrology: Gemini
Reversed: disconnected, unrealized partner
Musings: deep heart connections

VII Chariot

Qualities: gaining control, "getting one's act together," confidence, triumph, overcoming obstacles by will
Element: Water
Anatomy: chest
Astrology: Cancer
Reversed: a control freak
Musings: change, induced growth

VIII Strength

Qualities: asserting will, power, strong desires, intense emotions, courage to take risks
Element: Fire
Anatomy: solar plexus
Astrology: Leo
Reversed: overpowering, overwhelming
Musings: lustful, passionate, exciting, and willful

IX Hermit

Qualities: going within to gain spiritual awareness, patience, prudence, introspection
Element: Earth
Anatomy: colon
Astrology: Virgo
Reversed: isolated, overcautious
Musings: finding answers within self

X Wheel of Fortune

Qualities: changing towards good fortune, turning point, laws of karma, fate and destiny
Element: Fire
Anatomy: thighs
Astrology: Jupiter
Reversed: stuck in a rut or old patterns
Musings: creative flow, things turning around

XI Justice

Qualities: deciding fairly, balance, harmony, law of cause and effect
Element: Air
Anatomy: kidneys
Astrology: Libra
Reversed: unfair, unjust
Musings: coming to center, just

XII Hanged Man

Qualities: turning things upside down, upended, unconventional behavior, pattern breaker
Element: Water
Anatomy: feet
Astrology: Neptune
Reversed: unwilling to see things differently
Musings: hung up, self-imposed suffering, liberation

XIII Death

Qualities: letting go and rebirth, renewal, transformation, an ending
Element: Water
Anatomy: genitals
Astrology: Scorpio
Reversed: resisting transformation
Musings: letting go, shedding an old skin

SHORT LISTS OF ELEMENTS, CHAKRAS, & TAROT CARDS

XIV Temperance

Qualities: balancing all elements, alchemy, compatibility, cooperation
Element: Fire
Anatomy: thighs
Astrology: Sagittarius
Reversed: imbalanced
Musings: artful, calm, centered

XV Devil

Qualities: looking at surface appearances, bedeviled, frustration, acting without awareness
Element: Earth
Anatomy: knees
Astrology: Capricorn
Reversed: overly dark and superficial
Musings: indulgent, sexual, exploring temptations

XVI Tower

Qualities: breaking down defenses and boundaries, an upheaval, bolt of insight, a catalyst
Element: Fire
Anatomy: forehead
Astrology: Mars
Reversed: total deconstruction, devastation
Musings: lightning striking, reclaiming authentic self, falling apart

XVII Star

Qualities: glowing inspiration, spiritual regeneration, purification, renewal
Element: Air
Anatomy: ankles
Astrology: Aquarius
Reversed: unrealized self-worth
Musings: confidence, self-respect, revealing self to others

XVIII Moon

Qualities: trusting your intuition, experiencing the unconscious, imagination, listening to your dreams
Element: Water
Anatomy: feet
Astrology: Pisces
Reversed: dismissing the unconscious and deep wisdom
Musings: answers through dreaming, true self, ultimate test of reclaiming self

XIX Sun ···

Qualities: Experiencing full happiness, clarity, health and vitality, wholeness
Element: Fire
Anatomy: solar plexus
Astrology: Sun
Reversed: shadowed
Musings: new vitality, pure exuberance

XX Judgment ··

Qualities: Awakening to something you have not seen before, a paradigm shift, liberation
Element: Water
Anatomy: genitals
Astrology: Pluto
Reversed: ignoring the call of Spirit
Musings: discernment, the alchemist

XXI World ···

Qualities: Dancing with your limitations and success
Element: Earth
Anatomy: knees
Astrology: Saturn
Reversed: hampered progress or failure
Musings: totality, union of all, creation

AIR CARDS – INTELLECTUAL LIFE

Chakra: heart
Anatomy: shoulders, kidneys, and ankles
Sense: touch
Body response: movement and speed
Emotions: compassion/desire
Color: green
Keywords: mental, thought, contemplate, ideas, movement, speed, disperse, lightness

Ace of Air ··

A clear message, a new idea, inspiration
Reversed: muddiness
Musings: focused thoughts

SHORT LISTS OF ELEMENTS, CHAKRAS, & TAROT CARDS

Two, Three, Four of Air
Sign: Libra, cardinal Air
Anatomy: kidneys
Touch: rocking

Two of Air
Characteristics: balancing thoughts, peace of mind, clear and cool minded
Quality: duality
Planet: Moon
Reversed: erratic thoughts
Musings: peace, stalemate, calm mind

Three of Air
Characteristics: quarreling, sorrow, heartbreak
Quality: ideas
Planet: Saturn
Reversed: releasing upset
Musings: reworking old issues, mental sorrow, obstacle to love

Four of Air
Characteristics: taking/needing time out, retreat
Quality: grounded
Planet: Jupiter
Reversed: pushing on without a break
Musings: truce, needing to forgive, hiding out

Five, Six Seven of Air
Sign: Aquarius, fixed Air
Anatomy: ankles
Touch: light or off the body

Five of Air
Characteristics: losing a battle, defeating thoughts, difficulty, fears
Quality: struggling
Planet: Venus
Reversed: frozen by fear
Musings: mental anxiety

Six of Air ···

Characteristics: moving away from danger towards something more peaceful, very focused and calm
Quality: controlling
Planet: Mercury
Reversed: miscommunication
Musings: acceptance, objectivity, reason

Seven of Air ···

Characteristics: sneaking around, feeling hopeless and overburdened, struggling
Quality: inner reflection
Planet: Moon
Reversed: denial
Musings: futility, sabotage, yes . . . but

Eight, Nine, Ten of Air
Sign: Gemini, mutable Air
Anatomy: shoulders
Touch: deep and dispersing

Eight of Air ···

Characteristics: feeling trapped, restricted, over-analyzing, victimhood
Quality: change
Planet: Jupiter
Reversed: seeing the way out
Musings: not seeing the big picture, negative thinking

Nine of Air ···

Characteristics: having nightmares, negative thinking
Quality: mind-chatter
Planet: Mars
Reversed: justifying negative thinking
Musings: self-deprecation and abuse

Ten of Air ···

Characteristics: over exaggerating, complete ruin, negative thoughts, martyrdom
Quality: lost cause
Planet: Sun
Reversed: exhausted by hitting rock bottom
Musings: negative drama

SHORT LISTS OF ELEMENTS, CHAKRAS, & TAROT CARDS

Art form: dance

King of Air – mature male – leads ···

Characteristics: warrior approach, aggressive, direct
Quality: focused
Sub-Element: Air
Reversed: unsympathetic, mean
Musings: idea person, implementer

Queen of Air – mature female – nurtures ···

Characteristics: fair, focused, objective, cool approach
Quality: clear
Sub-Element: Water
Reversed: unjust, deceitful
Musings: formal, intense, earnest

Knight of Air – young adult – seeks ···

Characteristics: independent, dynamic, speeds towards goal
Quality: intuitive
Sub-Element: Fire
Reversed: delusional, ruthless
Musings: quick fix, vigorous, compelling

Page of Air – childlike – learns ···

Characteristics: brainy, thoughtful, studious, serious
Quality: practical
Sub-Element: Earth
Reversed: lacking confidence, hurt
Musings: single-minded, bookish

FIRE CARDS – SPIRITUAL AND CREATIVE LIFE

Chakra: solar plexus
Anatomy: forehead, solar plexus, thighs
Sense: sight
Body response: shaking
Emotions: enthusiasm/anger
Color: yellow
Keywords: spiritual, create, insight, passion, brightness, action, focus, vitality

Ace of Fire

Passionate creativity, beginnings, intuition
Reversed: delayed growth or creativity
Musings: seed of passion and growth

Two, Three, Four of Fire

Sign: Aries, cardinal Fire
Anatomy: forehead
Touch: rocking

Two of Fire

Characteristics: integrating and balance, planning, power, preparation
Quality: duality
Planet: Mars
Reversed: imbalanced, unprepared
Musings: actions and passions begin to manifest

Three of Fire

Characteristics: solidifying ideas, virtue, opportunity
Quality: grouping
Planet: Sun
Reversed: inappropriate use of will
Musings: integrity, looking back to see what is ahead

Four of Fire

Characteristics: celebrating a happy home, rejoicing, solid passion, ideas
Quality: stability

Planet: Venus
Reversed: unrealized possibilities
Musings: new direction, solid

Five, Six, Seven of Fire

Sign: Leo, fixed Fire
Anatomy: solar plexus
Touch: light or off the body

Five of Fire

Characteristics: striving, an amusing challenge
Quality: struggles
Planet: Saturn
Reversed: antagonistic
Musings: sparring, anxious, frantic

Six of Fire

Characteristics: coming out ahead, victory
Quality: triumph
Planet: Jupiter
Reversed: fleeting or unrecognized achievement
Musings: success, win-win situation

Seven of Fire

Characteristics: finding courage, valor, defiance
Quality: accomplishments
Planet: Mars
Reversed: lack of courage
Musings: standing up for one's own beliefs

Eight, Nine, Ten of Fire

Sign: Sagittarius, mutable Fire
Anatomy: thighs
Touch: deep and dispersing

Eight of Fire

Characteristics: action, swiftness, travel
Quality: change

Planet: Mercury
Reversed: unable to act
Musings: zooming ahead, nothing stopping the flow

Nine of Fire ···
Characteristics: strengthening, endurance, resilience
Quality: culmination
Planet: Sun and Moon
Reversed: unrealized potential
Musings: coming out on the other side, success after a battle

Ten of Fire ···
Characteristics: becoming exhausted after a completed task and too many burdens
Quality: overabundance
Planet: Saturn
Reversed: denying burdens
Musings: burnt out, carrying a heavy load for too long

FIRE COURTS – SEEK A SPIRITUAL OR CREATIVE LIFE
Art form: visual art

King of Fire – mature male – leads ···
Characteristics: fertile, creative approach, has a vision, secure
Quality: vital
Sub-Element: Air
Reversed: arrogant, sharp tempered
Musings: makes things happen

Queen of Fire – mature female – nurtures ···
Characteristics: inspired, passionate, interested in spiritual growth, knows herself
Quality: transformative
Sub-Element: Water
Reversed: single minded, pushy
Musings: interested in spiritual growth, fertile, sexy

Knight of Fire – young adult – seeks ···
Characteristics: passionate, lustful, creative
Quality: inspired
Sub-Element: Fire
Reversed: zealous
Musings: strong, forceful

SHORT LISTS OF ELEMENTS, CHAKRAS, & TAROT CARDS

Page of Fire – childlike – learns ···
Characteristics: open and full of wonder, free, breaks obstacles
Quality: spontaneous
Sub-Element: Earth
Reversed: spoiled, bratty
Musings: athletic

WATER CARDS – EMOTIONAL LIFE

Chakra: sacral
Anatomy: chest, pelvis, feet,
Sense: taste
Body response: smooth and flowing
Emotions: letting go/attachment
Color: orange
Keywords: emotional, love, relationship, connect, flowing, receptive, nurturing, merging

Ace of Water ···
The beginning of love, emotional balance, open heart
Reversed: hypersensitive
Musings: pure love

Two, Three, Four of Water
Sign: Cancer, cardinal Water
Anatomy: chest, breast
Touch: rocking

Two of Water ···
Characteristics: beginning a new relationship, young lovers, feeling romantic
Quality: relationship
Planet: Venus
Reversed: unbalanced union
Musings: trustful heart

Three of Water

Characteristics: celebrating friendship, abundance, synthesis of love
Quality: collaboration
Planet: Mercury
Reversed: insincerity
Musings: ultimate joyous communication

Four of Water

Characteristics: withholding emotions, self-protective, safety
Quality: stagnation
Planet: Moon
Reversed: apathy, disinterest
Musings: closed-off heart, little hope

Five, Six, Seven of Water

Sign: Scorpio, fixed Water
Anatomy: pelvis
Touch: light or off the body

Five of Water

Characteristics: disappointing, loss, hope, sorrow
Quality: feeling alone
Planet: Mars
Reversed: despair
Musings: the cup is half empty, murky waters

Six of Water

Characteristics: giving and receiving pleasure, emotional sweetness, nostalgia
Quality: harmony, flow
Planet: Sun
Reversed: selfish
Musings: playful, giving from the heart, spontaneous, yet balanced joy

Seven of Water

Characteristics: indulging emotions, illusions, fears
Quality: self-reflection
Planet: Venus
Reversed: trapped in fantasies
Musings: "poor me," warning not to "go there"

Eight, Nine, Ten of Water

Sign: Pisces, mutable Water
Anatomy: feet
Touch: deep and dispersing

Eight of Water ···

Characteristics: walking away from a situation, seeking answers
Quality: change
Planet: Saturn
Reversed: irresponsible, prolonging difficulties
Musings: overwhelmed, leaving something behind

Nine of Water ···

Characteristics: embodying pleasure, emotional fulfillment, happiness
Quality: completion
Planet: Jupiter
Reversed: interested in superficial pleasures
Musings: content, satisfied

Ten of Water ···

Characteristics: overflowing with love, domestic contentment, satiety
Quality: overabundance
Planet: Mars
Reversed: discontent, bored
Musings: deep inner satisfaction, status quo

WATER COURT CARDS – SEEK AN EMOTIONAL LIFE

Art form: cooking

King of Water – mature male – leads ···

Characteristics: benevolent ruler, committed
Quality: loyal
Sub-Element: Air
Reversed: dishonorable, heartless, cruel
Musings: lover of life

Queen of Water – mature female – nurtures ·······································

Characteristics: psychic, intuitive, connects
Quality: integrity
Sub-Element: Water

Reversed: smothering, overbearing
Musings: warm, affectionate, caring

Knight of Water – young adult – seeks ······························
Characteristics: warm, loving, giving, sharing
Quality: desire
Sub-Element: Fire
Reversed: a seducer, wears heart on sleeve
Musings: pursues lovers and romance

Page of Water – childlike – learns ·····························
Characteristics: affectionate, fantasizes about love
Quality: non-possessive
Sub-Element: Earth
Reversed: hypersensitive
Musings: romantic dreamer

EARTH CARDS – PHYSICAL LIFE

Chakra: root
Anatomy: neck, colon, knees,
Sense: smell
Body response: contraction
Emotions: courage/ fear
Color: deep red
Keywords: physical, sense, work, money, structure, methodical, organized, grounded

Ace of Earth ···
A new enterprise or way of receiving money, planting a new seed for success, material foundation
Reversed: delayed success
Musings: a solid entrepreneurial idea

SHORT LISTS OF ELEMENTS, CHAKRAS, & TAROT CARDS

Two, Three, Four of Earth

Sign: Capricorn, cardinal Earth
Anatomy: knees
Touch: rocking

Two of Earth
Characteristics: change, equality
Quality: balance
Planet: Jupiter
Reversed: juggling too much
Musings: polarity, external change

Three of Earth
Characteristics: negotiating a business deal, working, apprenticeships
Quality: synthesizing work
Planet: Mars
Reversed: difficult negotiations
Musings: synthesizing, actualizing

Four of Earth
Characteristics: establishing a foundation, centered, solid, forceful, safe
Quality: stable
Planet: Sun
Reversed: ungrounded, limiting
Musings: holding on to what you have, protective

Five, Six, Seven of Earth

Sign: Taurus – fixed Earth
Anatomy: neck
Touch: light or off the body

Five of Earth
Characteristics: feeling left out in the cold, concerned about external things, worrying about health
Quality: conflict
Planet: Mars
Reversed: desolate
Musings: self-absorption, self-consciousness, hypochondria

Six of Earth ....

Characteristics: sharing successes, accomplishments, generosity, charity
Quality: exuberance, triumph
Planet: Moon
Reversed: denying needs of self or others
Musings: slow, steady success, reciprocity

Seven of Earth ....

Characteristics: fearing failure, slow to progress, waiting for growth
Quality: inner work
Planet: Saturn
Reversed: impatient
Musings: uncertain, limitations

Eight, Nine, Ten of Earth

Sign: Virgo, mutable Earth
Anatomy: colon
Touch: deep and dispersing

Eight of Earth ....

Characteristics: working hard, prudence, skills
Quality: change, inspiration
Planet: Sun
Reversed: exhausted, overworked
Musings: "nose to the grindstone," competent

Nine of Earth ....

Characteristics: enjoying resources, success, happy in one's garden
Quality: completion
Planet: Venus
Reversed: needy
Musings: materialistic content

Ten of Earth ....

Characteristics: wealth, prosperity
Quality: abundance
Planet: Mercury
Reversed: unsatisfied
Musings: high self-esteem

SHORT LISTS OF ELEMENTS, CHAKRAS, & TAROT CARDS

Art form: sculpture, aromatherapy

King of Earth – mature male – leads ·······································

Characteristics: solid approach, concerned with finances, authoritative, stable
Quality: prosperous
Sub-Element: Air
Reversed: arrogant, miserly
Musings: practical, honest, sincere

Queen of Earth – mature female – nurtures ·······························

Characteristics: interested in community, protective, Mother Earth
Quality: health conscious
Sub-Element: Water
Reversed: sluggish, stagnant
Musings: takes physical care of others, kind

Knight of Earth – young adult – seeks ·································

Characteristics: slow steady movement, healer
Quality: builder, athlete
Sub-Element: Fire
Reversed: stubborn, entitled
Musings: methodical yet slow to action

Page of Earth – childlike – learns ······································

Characteristics: births new forms, creative learner
Quality: precocious
Sub-Element: Earth
Reversed: sophomoric
Musings: committed to studying

Please note that the Major Arcana cards references ascend upwards from the Throat/ Ether Chakra.

I – VII RELATES TO THE ETHER CHAKRA
VIII – XIV RELATES TO THE THIRD EYE CHAKRA
XV – XXI RELATES TO THE CROWN CHAKRA

The Crown Chakra
"I understand."

Shasrara, or "one thousand," is what the Crown Chakra is called in Sanskrit. This means "infinity" and describes the one-thousand petals (of consciousness vibration) ascribed to this "lotus." Located at the top of the head, it is the point where energy flows into the entire Chakra system from cosmic source. The Crown Chakra has the lightest, finest, and highest frequency/vibration.

The color most often associated with the Crown Chakra is violet. Some sources say the color is gold, or simply white light. The Crown Chakra does not relate to a specific element; instead, it corresponds to consciousness of peace and purity. There is no sound for the Crown Chakra, but only the absence of sound – so its sound quality is silence, the creative matrix of sound from which all other sounds are created. The main function of the Crown Chakra is to bring conscious, spiritual liberation, enabling you to obtain your purest essence. The Crown Chakra draws energy into our bodies from the rest of the universe. It connects to the divine on a cosmic scale. It is the ultimate experience of Spirit in and as the body.

THE THREE UPPER CHAKRAS &
THE MAJOR ARCANA CARDS

This Chakra is about being present, and truly letting go. It contributes to healing and feeling whole. The Crown Chakra is associated with the planet Uranus that frees us from limitations. The physical gland that corresponds to the Crown Chakra is the pineal gland. This gland's functions are somewhat of a mystery. It produces melatonin that helps with sleep and the development of other glands. The pineal gland might have something to do with psychic development.

In a sense, experiencing the Crown Chakra is much like what Abraham Maslow (1908–1970) regarded as peak experience. Maslow, the renowned psychologist and writer, researched what he called peak experiences. These are experiences where there are sudden feelings of intense well-being, and even a possible awareness of the ultimate happiness. He says these experiences are rare and mystical. People who have them are usually emotionally healthy. They tend to become more loving and accepting. Maslow believed peak experiences proved the vast capacities of the human mind.

CROWN CHAKRA/MA XV–XXI SUIT SELF-SOOTHER

Keep one end of the hand lightly on the top of your head and over your forehead with or without actually touching. Invoke clarity and connection to the universe. After a few minutes, when you can feel the pulses resonanate, move both hands to the top of the head.

MAJOR ARCANA CARDS XV–XXI

The Crown Chakra represents the last of the seven Major Arcana cards: XV Devil, XVI Tower, XVII Star, XVIII Moon, XIX Sun, XX Judgment, XXI World.

These cards relate to the experiences known as subconscious archetypical experiences. They are the deepest and most ethereal and cosmic of all experiences.

Third Eye Chakra
"I see."

The Third Eye Chakra is about inner vision. It is the "Seat of Wisdom" and is called "Ajna" in Sanskrit, which means "perception" or "command center." The Third Eye Chakra is located in the middle of the forehead. It is related to the color indigo. Instead of correlating to an element, it is said to correspond to light itself, because it generates and processes a large spectrum of electromagnetic rays. This is where psychic abilities are experienced, enabling one to see as if with a "third eye." These abilities, whether innate, learned, or resulting from trauma, need to be trained and developed by means of philosophical and spiritual work, ideally including practices such as chanting, yoga, or meditation. The Third Eye Chakra can connect us to the recognition and manifestation of synchronous events in our outer worlds.

The Third Eye or Brow Chakra correlates to the planet Jupiter. Jupiter is an expansive influence and emphasizes truth. The pituitary gland is housed in this Chakric center, and aids in influencing and regulating the other glands. Its function is important in maintaining well-being.

THIRD EYE CHAKRA/MA VIII–XIV SUIT SELF-SOOTHER

Rub both hands together until you feel heat. Cupping your hands slightly, place them over your forehead and eyes. Move your hands very slowly in a circle. Feel the warmth from your hands. Imagine light energy coming from your hands. Ask for clarity of purpose.

MAJOR ARCANA VIII – XIV

Third Eye cards are VIII Strength, IX Hermit, X Wheel of Fortune, XI Justice, XII Hanged Man, XIII Death and XIV Temperance.

Third Eye cards are in the middle of the Major Arcana line up. They signify archetypical experiences belonging to the unconscious mind. They are less qualitative experiences, and require an inner knowing.

The "third" or "inner" eye can see things our two mundane, physical eyes do not. Kabbalists wore a talisman of a third eye tied to a red string. Called "roite bindele," it was worn on the left wrist to ward off evil spirits.

THE THREE UPPER CHAKRAS &
THE MAJOR ARCANA CARDS

The Ether Chakra governs the faculty of communication and assists in finding one's true voice. Located in the throat, it is the juncture between our spiritual self and our physical self. In a sense, the Ether (or Throat) Chakra connects the tangible body to the Spirit body. The Sanskrit name is "Vishuddha," which means "purification," and is associated with the color blue. The qualities and experiences are of sound and space. The specific sound vocalization to use to engage the Ether Chakra is "Ham." The symbol is an inverted triangle surrounded by a circle.

The Ether Chakra relates to the planet Mercury, which represents communication and skill. It is associated with the thyroid gland that helps with metabolism, how the body breaks down food.

ETHER CHAKRA/MA I–VI SUIT SELF-SOOTHER

Keep your hands soft and relaxed. The touch is light. Allow your hands to go around the back of your neck, crossing at the occipital ridge. Your thumbs should rest by the side of the neck. Send an intention of allowing more space and understand of archetype experiences.

MAJOR ARCANA CARDS I–VII

Ether Cards are I Magician, II High Priestess, III Empress, IV Emperor, V Hierophant, VI Lovers, and VII Chariot.

Ether Chakra Cards have to do with external and tangible qualities that everyone may experience. They are simple and clear. They encourage us to be conscious about what is going on.

Major Arcana Card Meanings

The Fool card stands alone, in a category of its own, representing everything or nothing.

0 FOOL

Sub-Element: Air
Astrology: Uranus – free from limitations
Anatomy: ankles

Attributes: The Fool is spontaneous and seeks adventure. He is the archetypal wanderer and risk-taker. He is guileless. The Fool is both unconstrained and unrestrained.

Advice: Go on a whim or take a leap of faith. Just go. Be brave and open to anything new. Find your truth and see where it leads you.

Story: The meaning of the Fool has evolved. At points, he was seen as rash and goofy. In medieval kingdoms, the Jester, who had qualities of the "Wise Fool," served the court in the role of a clown or trickster. Jesters entertained the king, but also satirized corruption, hubris, or arrogance on the part of the rulers. They also had privileges and duties that included speaking the truth to their employers, even if it was critical or unwelcome.

The Fool is the Joker in a deck of playing cards. He can manifest as anything. Today, the Fool is admired and respected. He is still carefree, yet his risk-taking is viewed more as a choice and courage. The Fool is the only card that does not belong to one particular Chakra.

The Fool is the first of the Major Arcana cards and represents the soul embarking upon journey. If the soul survives intact, it is housed in a cave behind the heart. If not, due to trauma or other injuries to Spirit, it can take refuge in other, hidden areas of the body consciousness. If this is the case, it requires "soul retrieval," trauma release, or other somatic therapeutic healing methods in order to become re-integrated and restored to wholeness. To my mind, it makes sense that the Fool energy, or archetypical, free or a prior "soul" would normally abide below the Ether Chakra and above (or behind) the Air Chakra.

THE THREE UPPER CHAKRAS &
THE MAJOR ARCANA CARDS

I MAGICIAN

Sub-Element: Air
Astrology: Mercury – verbal expression
Anatomy: shoulders

Attributes: The Magician knows what he wants and how to get it in an organized fashion. He does what needs to be done with confidence. The Magician combines information with effort and intention. He is articulate and technically skilled.

Advice: You have all the tools you need to make something transpire or happen. Focus and actualize. Become an expert like magic. Just do it.

Whenever you have an especially auspicious occasion, a magical moment, or a simple synchronistic event, express it in some way. Tell it to a friend or write it down to validate what happened. This completes the circuit of energy and leads to more magical moments.

Story: Hart's life was over in her hometown. All her relatives had died in this place, where her family had lived for three generations. Her career and friendships seemed to be dissolving. It took all her tenacity to break away.

Hart had to be organized and communicate to get help. She had to let go and sell family heirlooms, find a property manager for the rental building, close down her business, physically pack and move, and find a new place to live in a part of the country where she had no ties or connections. There was a lot to do on many levels but Hart made it happen.

II HIGH PRIESTESS

Sub-Element: Water
Astrology: Moon – emotional
Anatomy: feet

Attributes: The High Priestess is a calm, sensitive, and reflective influence. She is gentle and empathetic. She is the Goddess, connected to the ideas of wisdom and caring. The High Priestess has spiritual wisdom and speaks the truth. She sometimes appears detached because she directs her attention inward. She reminds us to be aware of rhythms within our bodies and the cycles of the moon.

Advice: Recognize your emotional needs and follow your instincts. Attend to your spiritual needs and then be supportive to others. Record your dreams. They are the key to unseen changes.

Story: To me, the High Priestess represents the most spiritual aspect of Mother Mary in Christianity. As I was raised Jewish, Mary, the Mother of Jesus, was not included in my religious training. My first introduction to Mary was a statue of her in a stone enclosure in the yard of the neighborhood Catholic Church. I was curious and began visiting her by myself.

Years later, as an adult, I went back to visit the statue. I was amazed to find a huge chunk of rose quartz above the enclosure. In my youth, I was not aware that rose quartz represented love, but in adulthood, this knowledge came to me. Mary remains close to my heart to this day.

THE THREE UPPER CHAKRAS &
THE MAJOR ARCANA CARDS

III EMPRESS

Sub-Element: Earth
Astrology: Venus – compassion
Anatomy: neck

Attributes: The Empress is the quintessential nurturer. She takes care of and loves others as if they were her own children. She is Mother Earth. She is altruistic, strong, and secure. She represents unconditional love and sympathy. She is proficient and kind.

Advice: Be open to receiving as much as giving. Know that your current situation has support behind it. Bless all that is beneficent in your life and feel gratitude.

Story: As children, we frequently visited my father's mother. My siblings, cousins, her own six children, and I called her Mom. Although she was poor, she would always feed us and give us candy and corny presents. Mom would prepare a huge pot of boiled chicken and bake cakes topped with leftover cake crumbs. Whatever she cooked tasted great because it was made with love. I treasured the small packaged toys that were bought in the five-and-dime store. We were fed with unconditional love.

IV EMPEROR

Sub-Element: Fire
Astrology: Aries – assertive
Anatomy: forehead

Attributes: The Emperor is a protector and a father figure. He provides for others. He is an extrovert. The Emperor is the expression of archetypical masculinity. He is not power hungry or obtuse but you cannot ignore him. He sets a good example for others to follow.

Advice: Be confident that the present challenges are being handled positively and in a timely manner. Make the best choice with faith. Be proud. Take control and trust.

Story: When I was a child it seemed all fathers wore overcoats and hats. They all looked the same to me, big and powerful. My father would work late into the evening, and I hardly got to see him. I was afraid I wouldn't be able to recognize him in public. In a sense, I was afraid of him. I knew he loved and provided for the family and I was in awe of what he represented.

THE THREE UPPER CHAKRAS &
THE MAJOR ARCANA CARDS

V HIEROPHANT

Sub-Element: Earth
Astrology: Taurus – secure
Anatomy: neck

Attributes: The Hierophant represents the didactic encounter between teacher and student. He embodies tradition and law, including the spiritual, cultural, and scientific. He represents exchanging knowledge and helping. The Hierophant recognizes the importance of fundamentals.

Historically, the Hierophant was represented by the Pope. He is wise and disciplined. He is resistant to novelty and is not easily swayed. Perhaps today, the Hierophant appears more as a guru or teacher in a mentor relationship.

Advice: Realize that you are in a teaching and learning relationship. Perhaps you are gaining knowledge or building a traditional foundation. Let the Hierophant help you understand all aspects of a particular topic. Teachers are always learning from their students.

Story: Matthew has been a university art history professor for over twenty-five years. He finds what the Hierophant offers to be oppressive. Matthew has always had to fight with the university administration to teach his view of art history.

On the other hand, with my own tendency toward non-linear approaches and perspectives, I find what the Hierophant has to offer to be a relief, refreshing. He helps by giving me the structure to gain clarity with what, and how, I'd like to express.

VI LOVERS

Sub-Element: Air
Astrology: Gemini – changeable
Anatomy: shoulders

Attributes: The Lovers represent not only sexual lovers, but also complementary partnerships of all kinds. It suggests a full understanding between two people. The Lovers perceive others as equal. The Lovers card signifies sharing, accepting, appreciating, and communicating. It indicates a state of emotional, spiritual, and psychological connectedness.

Advice: You are about to enter, or already have begun, a loving partnership. Learn to recognize what an equal relationship feels like. Treat a business colleague or any relationship with egalitarian respect. Love yourself first and foremost.

Story: My parents met on a blind date. My father's cousin, Stanley, and my mother's friend, Sylvia, were dating, and arranged for my father and mother to meet. Before my parents ever met, they both had a dream of moving to the other side of the George Washington Bridge and raising a family. It was love at first sight. They both knew they could make an equal partnership.

My parents were married fourteen months later and moved to New Jersey. They never stopped loving each other.

THE THREE UPPER CHAKRAS &
THE MAJOR ARCANA CARDS

VII CHARIOT

Sub-Element: Water
Astrology: Cancer – compassionate
Anatomy: pelvis

Attributes: The Chariot represents a calm and confident way of taking control. It is determined and steadfast, and takes the initiative. The Chariot overcomes inertia and helps you to connect. It is consistent and focused on overcoming obstacles.

Advice: Take the reins in your hands and control the journey of the Chariot. Stand up for your own beliefs. This takes effort and control.

Story: Ancient Egyptian tombs depict reliefs of warriors riding into battle on chariots drawn by horses. Historians believe that the chariot was the key to an Egyptian pharaoh's military success. The pharaoh's men first borrowed the domestication of horses from their neighbors. They then built sophisticated chariots, designed for efficiency and speed, to be pulled by the horses. The invention of the chariot revolutionized technology, and led the Egyptians to victory.[1]

VIII STRENGTH

Sub-Element: Fire
Astrology: Leo – proud
Anatomy: solar plexus

Attributes: Strength demands control by using personal dominance and will. It is tenacious and lustful. Strength won't be deterred or outsmarted. Strength is courageous, dominant, and unwavering. Strength is passionate and forceful.

Advice: Gather up your forceful energy – your passion, tenacity, and courage. Use this to take responsibility for your actions. Experience dominance by using mind over matter. This quality of Strength is different than the control of the Chariot. Strength functions by the Fire quality instead of by means of the Water element.

Story: In the literary tale, *Life of Pi*, a teenage boy is trapped on a lifeboat with a Bengal tiger. In order to survive, and to also save the tiger, Pi relies on the knowledge he's gained through exploring religions, and the lessons his father taught him about wild animals, to demonstrate utmost strength and tenacity. He manages to find food to feed the tiger and himself. Pi keeps the tiger at bay, successfully preventing the animal from attacking him during their shared ordeal, remaining safe and in control until they reach land.[2]

THE THREE UPPER CHAKRAS &
THE MAJOR ARCANA CARDS

IX HERMIT

Sub-Element: Earth
Astrology: Virgo – order
Anatomy: colon

Attributes: The Hermit needs solitude for introspection and the search for inner truth. He is a loner, and represents the need to withdraw from mundane life to reconsider and evaluate his existence for clearer understanding. The Hermit offers validation for meditation, thought, and looking inward. He is relevant, meaningful, and silent.

Advice: In order to gain spiritual awareness, look inward. Be prudent and patient. Take time for reflection. Get away from your busy life, literally or metaphorically. Do not be afraid to be alone.

Story: My friend, Joseph, owns land in the countryside, completely surrounded by woods. He knows his creeks and hills very well. He can stay on his property alone for days and be perfectly content, sleeping and cooking and working the land in all sorts of weather. He always comes back to the city renewed. It is his form of hermitage.

X WHEEL OF FORTUNE

Sub-Element: Fire
Astrology: Jupiter – expansion
Anatomy: thighs

Attributes: The Wheel of Fortune suggests a turn of events. It is active, unpredictable, and surprising. It is benevolent, lighthearted, and very thrilling. Fortune is inviting and desirable. It signifies the possibility of change and good fortune.

Advice: Something is about to change, most likely for the better. If you recognize and acknowledge this, your opportunities will come more easily. Enjoy the process. Examine your benefits with glee.

Story: For many years, I spent summers with a group of friends up in the Catskill Mountains in a house believed by the locals to be haunted. The ghosts liked us. We felt so safe that we left the doors unlocked while we went out to explore the countryside.

One day, after we all returned home, one of the housemates noticed her overnight bag had been unzipped and was lying open. All the possessions she'd packed in it, including photo equipment and clothing that she had brought in the bag, were still there. The only thing missing was a recently purchased, and somewhat pricey, china cup.

Since we couldn't find the cup anywhere, I pulled out my Rider/Waite Tarot deck for a consultation. When the Wheel of Fortune turned up, I knew the cup would show up as well. A few hours later one of the dogs came running into the house with the cup in his mouth. The cup had a small red devil on the handle, which looked exactly like the devil on the Rider/Waite image of the Wheel of Fortune.

Did whoever took it get scared of the ghosts and bring the cup back to the property? There was no way the dog could have gotten into the bag. To this day no one knows what really happened. Did reading the cards change our fortune?

THE THREE UPPER CHAKRAS &
THE MAJOR ARCANA CARDS

XI JUSTICE

Sub-Element: Air
Astrology: Libra – balance
Anatomy: kidneys

Attributes: Justice is fair, deliberate, and precise. Justice is neither kind nor cruel. She does not play favorites. Justice weighs the evidence, compares the facts, and comes to a conclusion. She is astute and honorable.

Advice: Weigh the possibilities. Come to your center: feel for, and find, the correct balance of fairness. If you are at a crossroads, choose which way is the right way for you. Some decisions are out of our hands. Accept and trust that everything is a process.

Story: Daniel, a Haitian photographer, was in Haiti during the 2010 earthquakes. Daniel took hundreds of photographs and posted thirteen of them on Twitter/twitpic. Major newspapers took his photos without permission and used them for their newspaper headline stories. Daniel sued all of the newspapers, and after four years of legal battles, he is winning his cases. The Internet makes us question rights of property laws. With the availability of information via the Internet, open access versus copyright law is up for debate. The choice between freedom of speech and censorship has taken on new meaning. When is it appropriate to use someone's images? At what point does downloading material become inappropriate and what should the consequences be? What's right? Who gets to decide?

XII HANGED MAN

Sub-Element: Water
Astrology: Neptune – spiritual realization
Anatomy: feet

Attributes: The Hanged Man is surprising, absolute, unexpected, and demanding. He is enlightened, unconventional, and liberated. The Hanged Man is also prudent and pragmatic. He looks at things differently. He hangs upside down, so he has a different perspective. He shakes things up and gets you to view things differently. The Hanged Man signifies a radical shift of perception. He is the pattern disruptor.

Advice: Expect the unexpected. In order to make a change, a particular pattern must be disrupted and then reorganized. You are ready to see things in a new way or from a different perspective. If your particular situation has been turned upside down, set the intention for the highest good. Change can only happen in the absence of controlling, habitual patterns.

Story: Hans Jenny (1904–1972), a physician and natural scientist, experimented with how patterns change with the change of a frequency sound (vibration). He placed sand on metal plates and when he tapped the edge of the plate with a particular note from a tuning fork, the sand formed a mandala pattern.

If the plate is tapped with a different tuning fork, another mandala pattern eventually forms. In between the two different mandala patterns the sand lost form and got jumbled. This is called a pattern disruption. Jenny's sand experiment is analogous to what happens when a behavioral pattern changes.[3]

THE THREE UPPER CHAKRAS &
THE MAJOR ARCANA CARDS

XIII DEATH

Sub-Element: Water
Astrology: Scorpio – deep
Anatomy: pelvis

Attributes: Death is a transformation and a letting go. The card may also indicate an illness. Occasionally, the Death card signifies an actual death. It is always a loss of some kind, and is only frightening when resisted. Death sheds, converts, and reveals.

Advice: The loss or ending you are experiencing is best viewed as a change and a cleansing. It will be replaced by something more suited to your evolving needs and bring a sense of new life, or rebirth. Even though everything eventually transforms, it is the unknown aspect that is curiously difficult.

Give yourself space to grieve whatever, or whomever, has passed. We learn so much about living from the dying. Set your intentions high and tell your stories.

Story: The astrological sign associated with Death is Scorpio. In many cultures, November first, right in the middle of Scorpio, is celebrated as the Day of the Dead. In Mexico, on the Day of the Dead, people create altars and visit the souls of their loved ones in cemeteries. The celebrations have become quite festive and the altars have been recognized as fine works of art.

XIV TEMPERANCE

Sub-Element: Fire
Astrology: Sagittarius – idealistic
Anatomy: thighs

Attributes: Temperance is calm, contained, and balanced. S/he is non-dramatic. To some, s/he may even manifest as dull. Temperance indicates a healing angel. S/he shows moderation and patience. Temperance can be subtle yet profound.

Advice: You are protected against any harmful negativity. You have an opportunity to heal and revitalize. It seems an outside force is protecting you.

Story: Healing is different from curing. Curing is the job of medical professionals. Healing, on the other hand, has become the job of alternative practitioners and spiritual counselors, like Tarot card readers.

I provided Polarity sessions for the AIDS community in NYC as part of my training. At the time, I heard the following example that exemplifies the difference between healing versus curing:

If you come home and you find your house has been robbed, you report it to the police, who then find the robbers, and you get all your stuff back. You've been "cured." But if every time you walk in your front door, you re-experience the same reactions you had when walking in after the robbery, you need to be healed. If you stay with the feelings triggered by your reaction, and work through those, even older issues will often turn out to have been healed.

THE THREE UPPER CHAKRAS &
THE MAJOR ARCANA CARDS

XV DEVIL

Sub-Element: Earth
Astrology: Capricorn – cautious
Anatomy: knees

Attributes: The Devil card influence is superficial, self-indulgent, and tends towards addictions. He is peculiar, and at times disastrous, even evil or perverted. The Devil is materialistic. He only sees surface appearances. The Devil is dark and obsessive, and lacks a sense of boundaries. He is bedeviled and can be rambunctious.

Advice: Look beyond surface appearances, indulgences, and behaviors that are ultimately counter-productive. Beware of all temptations. What problems do you need to address? Better boundaries need to be made.

Story: When William and Monica got married, I couldn't figure it out. They seemed ill-suited for one another. William was casual, youthful at heart, and didn't care as much about status as did Monica. He was thrilled that someone as beautiful as Monica wanted him. I thought she was a snob.

Shortly after their daughter was born, Monica insisted they move out to the suburbs, away from the city, William's friends, and work. William went along with the move. At one point, Monica insisted William buy an expensive new car, even though William liked his beat-up station wagon. William bought the car Monica wanted him to buy.

Eventually, Monica and William got divorced. I think the last straw was Monica wanting to redo the backyard on one of those TV redo shows, which removed William's basketball court. Monica is now remarried to a doctor and William moved to the city. His friends are glad to have him back.

XVI TOWER

Sub-Element: Fire
Astrology: Mars – drive
Anatomy: forehead

Attributes: The Tower is a disruption, a total breakdown. This card indicates a situation when nothing can possibly get worse. The tower indicates chaos and represents some ugly characteristics, and yet is at the core of victory and survival. It is inexorable and powerfully destructive of old, rigid, calcified forms that can no longer accommodate our growth or evolution.

Advice: You are in for a powerful shock or surprise. The benefit of this is that in the middle of chaos, you can experiment with new conditions. Look ahead and make room. It is the catalyst that gets us to change. Stay present with the disruption. It is only when things fall apart that they can be put back together again in a new way.

Story: The Tower of Babel is the Biblical story about a time when all the people on Earth spoke the same language. People worked to build a monumental tower to heaven to prevent their city from being scattered. God saw this as a point where people would eventually be lead away from God and create unity among each other. God destroyed the Tower in order to confuse their language, so they would not understand each other. The Bible explains that this is where separate cultures came into existence.

THE THREE UPPER CHAKRAS &
THE MAJOR ARCANA CARDS

XVII STAR

Sub-Element: Air
Astrology: Aquarius – independent
Anatomy: ankles

Attributes: The Star is glowing, optimistic, and charismatic. She represents hope and balance. The Star signifies the essence of spiritual regeneration. She is confident and pure in both her inner and outer qualities. She is about being peaceful and inspired. The Star is where dreams come true.

Advice: Getting the Star card does not mean becoming a celebrity. It is to be accepted and acknowledged as bringing inspiration and the renewal of inner and outer spiritual and artistic qualities. The Star card suggests that astral understandings and greater patterns of meaning are being channeled to you from the celestial realm of the Greater (or "Higher") Self.

Story: Jerry has been in and out of politics his whole life. One time, I saw him on an almost desolate street. He wasn't in the public eye, yet he glowed. I could see him a block away.

I experienced my own Star quality at my launch party for my *Polarity Wellness Tarot* deck. I gave a presentation about something that has never existed before, and was able to spontaneously relay very clearly. I was told that I glowed. I looked and felt great. Finally, I was coming into my own.

XVIII MOON

Sub-Element: Water
Astrology: Pisces – merging
Anatomy: feet

Attributes: The Moon is intuitive, cyclical, and connects us to subconscious levels of knowing, as well as to the collective unconscious. The Moon tells us to reflect on our dreams. The Moon card might suggest lunar "madness," or "lunacy," but there is always some truth to her perceptions.

The other side of the Moon is deceptive, disgraceful, and tricky. The Moon may refer to the occult.

Advice: The power of your unconscious mind will guide you. To find inner wisdom we must reclaim our true selves. We all experience natural change, just as the day follows the night and the moon changes from new to full.

This is a card with a dual meaning. On one hand, it indicates going into the dark and spooky unseen world. It might even indicate lunacy. On the other hand, the Moon illuminates the darkness, accessing deep, subconscious levels of intuition and psychic knowing.

Story: Marie prefers to live in this other reality filled with magic and taking care of animals. The deeper meaning behind everything is important to her. She is extremely sensitive and dreamy. She often telephones me just when a guest has arrived, like she knows someone is there.

Because of her life experience, this state is where Marie feels safe. She much prefers to stay awake late at night to either write or paint.

THE THREE UPPER CHAKRAS &
THE MAJOR ARCANA CARDS

XIX SUN

Sub-Element: Fire
Astrology: Sun – radiant
Anatomy: solar plexus

Attributes: The Sun betokens happiness and the sunny state of affairs whereby everything is going one's way. The card expresses health and vitality. The Sun is about being friendly, excited, outgoing, and blissful. The Sun card is an indication that you are in a truly good place.

Advice: Feel the power of complete happiness. Let the sun shine on you. Embrace it with grace and dignity. Check out how your life has evolved. Dispel any self-doubt. Nothing can go wrong.

Story: Mimi was in a really good place. She was finishing writing a book on a topic that she was creating, something she was told she would be doing years ago and could not imagine.

Mimi was also tapping into a magical place in her healing practice that she had not been at in years. She had lots of friends and a man who loved her. Mimi felt gratified in a way that she hadn't ever felt before.

XX JUDGMENT

Sub-Element: Water
Astrology: Pluto – transforming
Anatomy: genitals

Attributes: Judgment brings things to the light. It represents an *aha* moment. This indicates an awakening to something you have not seen before. Judgment signifies a paradigm shift or coming to your true self. Judgment is the angel of resurrection.

Advice: Wake up. Be present. You have come to a startling or transfiguring revelation. This is the vehicle for true change. Follow it as if Spirit was calling you. See the light and move forward.

Story: I taught visual arts in various capacities while living in NYC. I found the best way to teach a new concept or technique was to first present a visual challenge with shown examples. Then, with specific materials and/or format, I would allow my students to creatively solve the problem. As the students were working, I'd go around the room and give individual guidance. Whenever a student came to an understanding, I was convinced I heard a light bulb switch on in their head. The student had finally understood how to solve the problem, and sometimes made a great piece of art.

THE THREE UPPER CHAKRAS &
THE MAJOR ARCANA CARDS

XXI WORLD

Sub-Element: Earth
Astrology: Saturn – responsibility
Anatomy: knees

Attributes: The World card represents the ultimate experience. It means success and arrival. The World card signifies fulfilled dreams, accomplishments, and rewards. It indicates the place where you most are aligned with Spirit. This completion is dazzling and incredibly exciting.

Advice: Dance on your limitations. Take hold of the moment enjoy and celebrate. You are at the end of a cycle. Perform a ritual of gratitude.

Story: I met my first practicing Tibetan Buddhist while working at a community silkscreen studio in Manhattan during the '80s. Her project was to change a line drawing of a Tibetan village into a limited-edition silkscreen print on papyrus paper. The drawing had been made on site, in the pictured village. While we were working together, she shared her stories. At the time I didn't know how much Tibetan Buddhism would influence me thirty years later.

The only other card in Tarot to show a person in motion is the Fool card. After the World, we go back to the beginning, and once again meet the Fool. Some decks end with numbering the Fool as XXII, coming after the World card.

CHAPTER 7

Air Cards

AIR CHAKRA – "I LOVE."

The Air Chakra is commonly known as the Heart Chakra because it is located in the middle of the chest, near the heart. Our heart does much more than pump blood. It connects us to our emotions. The heart is the first organ in the body to develop. Gregg Braden, author and spiritual speaker, asks: "What it is that triggers the first heart beat?[1"]

As an organ develops, it sends electrochemical messages to the brain. As the heart develops, it begins to regulate the chemistry throughout the rest of the body. The heart sends the signals to the brain that trigger coherent feelings. This triggers a sense of peace, connectedness, trust, and wellbeing.

In 1998, the HeartMath Institute[2] published research on the power of the human heart to affect the mind and body. These scientists were able to measure the electromagnetic energy of the human heart with highly sophisticated equipment. They discovered that the energy field produced by the heart is far more powerful than anyone had previously imagined. They proved that the heart's electromagnetic energy field is as much as 5,000 times stronger than the energy field generated by your brain.

The Air Chakra is all about compassion, desire, and self-acceptance. It is the Chakra that is midway between the seven Chakras, and helps us to separate, as well as integrate.

The Sanskrit name for the Air Chakra is "Anahata," which means "unstuck." The color related to the Air Chakra is green. The symbol is a six-pointed star. It is correlated with Venus, the planet of love. The sound vocalization is "Yam." The gland associated with the Air Chakra is the thymus, which aids in immune system functioning. The planet Venus corresponds to the Air/Heart Chakra, bringing love and compassion.

THE AIR CHAKRA/SUIT

AIR CHAKRA/SUIT SELF-SOOTHER

Keep your hands soft and relaxed. The touch is light. Place one hand so that it is holding the neck and one hand on your heart, the Air Chakra. Gently rub your heart. Breathe and feel the quality of your breath. Calm any scattered thoughts or quick movements with a gentle cool lightness.

Air Cards – Intellectual Life

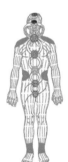

Chakra: heart
Anatomy: shoulders, kidneys, and ankles
Sense: touch
Body response: movement and speed
Emotions: compassion/desire
Color: green
Keywords: mental, thought, contemplate, ideas, movement, speed, disperse, lightness

Swords/Air cards signify everything mental. They are our thoughts, ideas, contemplations, and communication skills. In modern times, the Swords/Air cards have become related to computers and correspondences. They are most often depicted with swords as the elemental symbol, and sometimes with blades or, less often, birds. Movement, speed, and lightness are their characteristics. Swords/Air influence aspires to balance, justice, harmony, and diplomacy.

Swords/Air cards are about logic and the way we internalize negative and/or positive thinking. Swords/Air is the suit that has the most so-called "negative" cards. But it is also the suit that indicates thought patterns, which are the easiest patterns to change.

Swords/Air suit is about the way we make decisions and the ways in which we think. Change your thoughts; change your life. Most of our internal battles have to do with the way we think about things. Swords/Air cards can invoke curiosity, cleverness, apathy, or boredom.

ACE OF AIR

Quality: thinking
Signs: all Air signs – Gemini, Libra, Aquarius
Anatomy: all Air anatomy – shoulders, kidneys, ankles

Attributes: Ace of Air indicates a clear message and a new perspective. It signifies inspired ideas with easily reached solutions. The Ace of Air is focused and clear. It indicates the moment when the figurative light bulb goes off and illuminates our thoughts.

Advice: Develop the idea that inspires you. Stay focused. Notice where the clarity that begins to flower is located in your body. Anchor it so that next time, you will know if that sort of inspiration was a correct one to follow.

Story: The inspiration for creating my *Polarity Wellness Tarot* deck came from a conversation I had over dinner with my former Polarity teachers. I was telling them about a slide show I had developed with a colleague, showing world art images that related to the Tarot. I wasn't sure where we could take the presentation, or if it could sustain my colleague and myself. I was asking for advice.

They suggested creating a product. On the way home from dinner it became clear; I was going to create my own somatic tarot deck. Four years later, the deck was completed.

THE AIR CHAKRA/SUIT

Two, Three, Four of Air

Sign: Libra – Cardinal Air – balanced, just, harmonious, truth
Anatomy: kidneys
Touch: rocking

TWO OF AIR

Quality: duality
Planet: Moon – emotions, adaptable sense of self, reflective

Attributes: Two of Air is balanced, clear, and still. There is harmony and presence. It also indicates a calm, accepting peace of mind. Two of Air signifies complimentary or opposing thoughts held in a balanced equipoise. It means holding two disparate or contradictory ideas as true and valid at the same time. It also signifies the willingness to wait for more information to arrive before acting, if a choice or decision needs to be made.

Advice: Enjoy harmony of the mind when you have it. You cannot have happiness without sadness. Where is the feeling of peace in your body? Is it in your heart?

Story: I had a friend whom I felt I supported through some of her toughest times. I defended her when mutual friends criticized her. When it came time for her to be supportive of my projects, I felt she wasn't there. I was hurt, so I discussed this with her. My friend did not agree. She thought that I had another agenda. We agreed to disagree.

THREE OF AIR

Quality: ideas
Planet: Saturn – order, form, disciplined, fear, contraction, transcendence

Attributes: Three of Air is sorrowful, heartbreaking, and suggests a quarrel. It indicates confused and disappointing thoughts. Three of Air signifies depressive thoughts that fuel suffering. Three of Air shows a state of failing confidence or of being easily deterred, and may indicate an actual illness, usually due to stressful thoughts.

Advice: When your heart hurts, stay present and abide with it. Meditate or get a soothing bodywork session. Are your old issues resurfacing? Talk about what is going on for you, and notice what you are thinking and how these thoughts, fears, or memories make you feel.

Story: One winter when I was in high school, my family adopted an orange tabby cat who had been eating the fat trimmings from meat that my mother left out for the birds. We named him Rudolph because his nose was red due to the cold winter. Over the years, especially after all of us kids left for college, my mother grew to love that cat. She nurtured his injuries after cat fights and let him sleep in the house.

One time, when Rudolph got into a particularly bad catfight, my mother decided to take him to the vet. When she got to the parking lot of the vet's office, and went to take him out of the car, Rudolph jumped from her arms, never to be seen again. My Mother was so heartbroken. For years, she regretted losing him.

THE AIR CHAKRA/SUIT

FOUR OF AIR

Quality: grounded
Planet: Jupiter – truth, faith, grace, optimistic, expansive

Attributes: The Four of Air indicates patience and restfulness. It signals a period of retreating and waiting. The Four of Air means slowing down in order to regenerate and organize. It is a truce of some kind.

Advice: It is not a time to move forward or take any quick action. Sleep. Withdraw in order to recover. It is always easier to recover from an injury or emotional upheaval when the difficulty is recognized and addressed early. Meditate and rest. It is time to ground and regroup.

Story: When Lewis gets home from work, he slows down almost completely. At work he runs around nonstop. If he's not on the phone or helping customers in the shop, he is on the computer or checking on jobs that are being printed.

On the weekends, he sometimes stays in bed for the entire day. Lewis reads the paper or watches sports on TV. Even though he is not sick or interested in sleeping, he needs to get under the covers for rest and recovery.

Five, Six, Seven of Air

Sign: Aquarius – Fixed Air – trendsetter, extremist, individualistic
Anatomy: ankles
Touch: light or off the body

FIVE OF AIR

Quality: hopelessness
Planet: Venus – love

Attributes: Five of Air indicates a sense of failure, disappointment and/or cruelty. The Five of Air means difficulties and conflicts. It is disillusionment and regret.

Advice: Failing is easier if you can accept that it is part of growing and changing. It is the anticipation of failing that is difficult. It is time to move on. Nothing was ever created without mistakes. This card may also indicate not being equipped with the right tools yet. Find the courage to continue. Samuel Beckett may have said it best: "Ever tried. Ever failed. No matter. Try again. Fail again. Fail better."[3]

Story: Alice was stuck in traffic and late to pick up her kids. When she finally did pick them up, they were both cranky. She was tired and her back ached. Maybe she was coming down with the cold her son was just getting over.

When they got home Alice realized she had forgotten to take anything out of the freezer for dinner. She listened to her phone messages, one reminding her of her massage appointment, which she wouldn't be able to go to because of a meeting in her office the next morning. She still had to do homework with her kids, who were fighting. She called her husband to ask if he could pick up a pizza on his way home from work, but he wasn't picking up his phone calls. Alice thought not being able to reach her husband was happening way too often.

THE AIR CHAKRA/SUIT

SIX OF AIR

Quality: very focused, calm
Planet: Mercury – communication, reason, skill, intelligence, verbal expression

Attributes: Six of Air is safe, serene, and focused. It is about moving away from danger and towards a better place. Six of Air is inarticulate yet understanding. The Six of Air influence accepts help from others. It looks forward to what is ahead and is optimistic about the future.

Advice: Appreciate that difficulties are behind you. You no longer need to be self-conscious or hold onto prevailing negative thoughts. You are out of any danger.

Story: At times in my life when I did not know what step to take next; I asked the universe to "Show me the unmistakable sign."

When my siblings and I moved my mother out of her condo in Florida, I went to clean up her apartment. All her friends and our relatives were advising me to find renters. I wasn't so sure. I just couldn't picture how that could be managed, and none of us had an affinity with Florida. It wasn't until I got there that I realized how much work it was going to be. The potential tenant I'd been referred to wasn't calling me back, and I was hesitant because I heard she smoked cigarettes. In between packing up all of my mother's personal belongings, I kept asking for a clear sign. At one point, I went into the room facing the outer walkway, where the window was open. Someone was smoking on the upstairs walkway. The smell of burning tobacco was pouring into the room. I immediately closed the window. A few hours later, I went back and could still smell the smoke.

This was my sign not to rent, because we could never sell a place that smelled from cigarettes in humid Florida. I immediately consulted my siblings and we agreed to sell the apartment. Everything from then on went smoothly. Although we sold it for far less than what my mother bought it for, those particular apartments continue to go down in value and so we did far better than we would have, had we waited.

SEVEN OF AIR

Quality: overburdened, sneaking around
Planet: Moon – emotions, adaptable sense of self, reflective

Attributes: The Seven of Air is insolent and sneaky. It is furtive, unreliable, and without integrity of intent. The Seven of Air denies feeling outfaced, and attempts to do everything on its own. There is an aspect of self-protection, selfishness, bravado, or "faking it," expending effort to be self-sufficient so as not to be dependent upon others, and therefore vulnerable. There are issues of trust and trustworthiness associated with this card. It is also courageous.

Advice: Stop denying your situation. Seek help from others. You do not have to do it all on your own. Sneaking around is not going to do any good. Your life is wide open, in any event, and everyone sees your plight. Let go of your protectionist efforts, or of trying to "cover" for personal deficits or perceived inadequacies; cease your struggle to be "an island."

Story: When I first met Alan at a networking event, I was impressed that he expressed an interest in me. Alan ran a successful holistic health center where I dreamed of working. I thought he wanted to be friends. I was disappointed to realize Alan only wanted my personal business. Even though Alan is seemingly friendly, he really doesn't have many friends. He's kind of a shyster. I wonder what happened to him in his past.

THE AIR CHAKRA/SUIT

Eight, Nine, Ten of Air

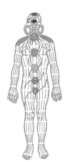

Sign: Gemini – Mutable Air – compassionate, sensitive, nurturing, protective, connecting mother to child
Anatomy: shoulders
Touch: deep and dispersing

EIGHT OF AIR

Quality: trapped in thoughts
Planet: Jupiter – truth, faith, grace, optimistic, expansive

Attributes: The Eight of Air can suggest a feeling of being trapped, blinded by anxiety, and therefore lacking in foresight. It betokens rigidity, martyrdom, and self-consciousness. The Eight of Air indicates rigid beliefs or fearfulness, and an inability to see the whole picture.

Advice: You are not as trapped as you think you are. Open your eyes and see your options. Look at things objectively. Have a sense of humor. Be open to new points of view.

Story: Katie used to live across the street. She's what I would call a fragile soul. She was friendly at first and then, one day, she stopped talking to me. She would hide if she saw me walking out my door. Katie never told me why she behaved the way she did, but eventually I heard I was not the only one she avoided. If there was something anyone said or did that didn't agree with her position, she thought they were her enemy.

One day, she just moved away. She didn't tell anyone except one neighbor who reported that she was glad to get away from all those horrible people. It is curious because it is a rather friendly neighborhood, but she was unable to perceive this.

NINE OF AIR

Quality: intense negative thinking
Planet: Mars – drive, desire, courage

Attributes: The Nine of Air card describes a condition of negative mind chatter, self-recrimination or doubt, and suffering. It is desolate and isolated. The Nine of Air indicates the condition of over obsessing on fearful, negative or anxious thoughts, to the point where those thoughts are start to infiltrate your dreams. It may indicate anger, depression, or excessive worrying.

Advice: Recognize your negative thought patterns and how they are affecting your life. Look at your situation objectively. Let the words go and release them. Give them space with your breath. Reflect on yourself. Be kind to yourself. Wake up every morning and make (or aspire to) something positive.

Story: Sarah still worried obsessively about the time her friend's family came from London to visit four years ago. Apparently, Sarah could not be as attentive as she would have liked. When she went to visit them, her itinerary was planned out for a week. Sarah still worried that she had let her friends down.

THE AIR CHAKRA/SUIT

TEN OF AIR

Quality: over dramatic
Planet: Sun – ego-identity, radiant Spirit, individuality

Attributes: Ten of Air tends to be overly dramatic and describes the perception of a completely devastating situation unfolding in one's life. The Ten of Air signifies the sense of defeat and ruin. It is ill luck or the culmination of failure. It tends to an over exaggeration of, and obsession with, the destructive elements in the situation. It also signifies the release, and letting go of what cannot work, making room for what can.

Advice: Do not allow your thoughts to become so devastating, and devastated, that you feel tortured. The message of this card tends to emphasize absolute destruction when in fact there are no absolutes. Breathe deeply into your core, and find positive thoughts.

Story: Sam is brilliant teenager. When he was a child, his teachers discovered that he was a gifted writer. Sam has had a far more difficult time than most teenagers. He has been diagnosed with all sorts of disorders. Mostly, he has trouble fitting in, and is unhappy. A few years ago, when he attempted suicide, he was put on medications. He also stopped writing.

A few months ago, Sam tried suicide again, this time over his mother refusing to allow him to get tattoos all over his body. Luckily, his attempt failed, but it sent him into the hospital for days. Something about this last incident changed Sam. Besides having his medication adjusted, Sam continues to get happier and is now writing a novel about his experiences.

SEEKS AN INTELLECTUAL LIFE

Art form: dance

KING OF AIR
Mature male – leads

Quality: focused
Sub-Element: Air

Attributes: The King of Air is cool-headed. He looks at things objectively and makes his decision from that basis. He's also very intelligent. He's a good communicator and can see through ideas to their core.

On the downside, he is heartless.

Advice: You are dealing with someone who is very professional and focused on what needs to get done. Don't take it too personally if he is critical or dispassionate in his dealing with you or your ideas.

Story: On the TV series *Star Trek: The Next Generation*, the character Jean-Luc Picard is the captain of the USS *Enterprise*. He has the clarity to get out of dangerous situations by keeping his cool. He is always fair and a no-nonsense kind of leader. He is always professional and rarely shows his emotions.[4]

THE AIR CHAKRA/SUIT

QUEEN OF AIR
Mature female – nurtures

Quality: clear
Sub-Element: Water

Attributes: The Queen of Air card brings energy that is objective yet fair. She has a cool approach. She has great ability to focus. She puts her emotions aside and gets straight to the point. The Queen of Air can also be clever and carry on an intellectual conversation. She is intense and earnest.

On the downside, she can be unjust and deceitful.

Advice: Be really clear with the Queen of Air and in using her energy or influence. She may be cool in her approach, but can help you cut through obstacles and obfuscation.

Story: When I worked at the community silkscreen studio in NYC, we hired an executive director to write grants and oversee the general management of the programs. We hired Sandra, who was an artist but not a printmaker. She was very competent at her job, but she was somewhat cold, and even seemed mean at times. What she really wanted was professionalism, but artists in a community arts studio setting aren't always ready for that.

KNIGHT OF AIR
Young adult – seeks

Quality: intuitive
Sub-Element: Fire

Attributes: The Knight of Air charges ahead with clear intent. He is sure of himself. He analyzes situations and is not very connected to his feelings. The Knight of Air may sometimes charge into decisions in haste. S/he may be looking for a quick fix. S/he is vigorous and compelling, independent, and dynamic.

On the downside, the Knight of Air can signify a ruthless and delusional approach.

Advice: Consider what you need to focus on and ask how to get the momentum to move quickly. Ask: Why am I charging ahead? Who is influencing me? Where does my focus belong?

Story: Admittedly, I am nonlinear by nature. The problem is that I live in a linear world. What I sometimes feel most comfortable doing is a type of multitasking. I'd rather call it collage mode.

Sometimes to get things done I'm better off doing a few things at once – especially if they are mundane tasks, boring, or something that I have not done before. If I have to clean my house, I sometimes would prefer cleaning while talking casually to a friend on the phone.

Doing more than one thing at a time gets me going and actually gets me to focus. Perhaps my unconscious mind likes to do things that way.

THE AIR CHAKRA/SUIT

PAGE OF AIR
Childlike – learns

Quality: practical
Sub-Element: Earth

Attributes: The Page of Air has a new idea. S/he is presenting a clear, logical thought. S/he has the ability to show how you communicate. The Page of Air is clear-sighted and brainy. S/he is serious.

On the downside the Page of Air lacks confidence and thinks too much.

Advice: Ask what is your new source of inspiration? Learn to stand up for yourself.

Story: Thomas has been playing computer games since he was about four years old. He has always been the baby of his family. He is now in college studying computer engineering.

His family never knew Thomas was so smart. Now he has been offered a highly paid internship. All his professors are impressed with his skills. He seems to be able to maintain an acute focus when needed. No one thinks of him as a baby anymore.

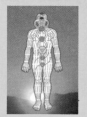

CHAPTER 8

Fire Cards

FIRE CHAKRA – "I DO."

The Fire Chakra reflects the strength of self-esteem, power, and enthusiasm, and governs the metabolic functions that supply physical energy in the form of heat. The Fire Chakra is located in our mid torso, at the base of our sternum and above our navel. This Chakra is commonly known as the solar plexus.

The Fire Chakra's color is yellow. This Chakra is symbolically expressed as an inverted triangle with ten lotus petals. In Sanskrit it is called "Manipura," meaning "city of gems." Its functions are associated with heat and light, fueling organs of digestion, assimilation, and energy conversion in the body. Psychologically and spiritually, this center governs the amount of passion, will, intent, integrity, right action, and courage available in the energy body. The traditional sound vocalization is "Ram."

The Fire Chakra is powerful and can be expressed in two extreme directions, as Mars-ruled drive or as anger and resentment. It influences your self-esteem. The Fire Element that governs this Chakra is the warmth and radiating energy from the sun. No wonder it is known as the solar plexus, which is the name given to the ganglion of nerves below the chest and above the stomach. The planetary influence of Mars gives drive and courage. The gland associated with the solar plexus is the pancreas. This gland aids in digestion and secretes enzymes that lower and regulate sugar levels in the body.

FIRE CHAKRA/SUIT SELF-SOOTHER

Place both hands over the abdomen, palms facing inward. Your thumbs and index fingers are touching. The touch is light. Imagine a mirror around your solar plexus. Imagine sending spontaneity and passion throughout your body.

THE FIRE CHAKRA/SUIT

Fire Cards - Spiritual and Creative Life

Chakra: solar plexus
Anatomy: forehead, solar plexus, thighs, sense of sight
Body response: shaking
Sense: sight
Emotions: enthusiasm, anger
Color: yellow
Keywords: spiritual, create, insight, passion, brightness, action, focus, vitality

Wands/Fire cards are creative and intuitive. They are about spontaneity and insight. Wands/Fire Suit is also called the suit of rods, staffs, batons or clubs. Fire can be associated with focusing energy and is the active, driving force behind anything we do.

The creative force of Wands/Fire mirrors the creative force deep within us. When we need it, Wands/Fire quality gives us confidence. It gives us fire to burn. It is our passion and our action.

Wands/Fire may also characterize egotistic identification and anger. Generally, Wands/Fire cards indicate outgoing, charismatic energy.

Wands/Fire influence is closely related to the spiritual life. Many of us who want meaning in our lives seek a spiritual path.

ACE OF FIRE

Quality: spiritual, creative
Signs: Aries, Leo, Sagittarius
Anatomy: forehead, solar plexus, thighs

Attributes: The Ace of Fire is the powerful seed of creativity. It is forceful, focused and passionate. The Ace of Fire is Spirit set into motion. It is intuitive.

Advice: Ignite your passion. Start that new project. Always create. It will open doors.

Story: When I was in art school, even though I was a printmaking major, I got more support from the photography department. It seemed logical that I might not have a print shop to work in after college, so I would take advantage of the facilities provided by the University and focus on printmaking.

During that time, I found myself most attracted to pop art by Andy Warhol and Robert Rauschenberg. I also found inspiration in any non-silver (not actual photographic) images. This existing art provided inspiration for my own creations.

THE FIRE CHAKRA/SUIT

Two, Three, Four of Fire

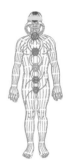

Sign: Aries – Cardinal Fire – focused on new experiences, active, outgoing, assertive, self-willed, starting things off
Anatomy: forehead
Touch: rocking

TWO OF FIRE

Quality: duality
Planet: Mars – drive, desire, courage

Attributes: The Two of Fire is the sprouting of a passion or Spirit. It indicates creative dualities brought together to reflect and animate each other. The Two of Fire is beauty and kindness. It is spiritually looking in the right direction. It ignites passion for a creative project, fuels it, and keeps it going. Aleister Crowley, who created the *Thoth* deck, referred to Two of Fire as Dominion.

Advice: Look back and see the patterns that have worked before. Begin to shed light onto a new project. Set forth a new challenge. Give that project new meaning.

Story: The Magritte painting(s), *Dominion of Light* (1953–1954), evokes the mystery of placing ordinary objects in an unusual context. René Magritte (1898–1967) is considered one of the most well-known Surrealist painters. Having an innovative vision is what makes *Dominion of Light* still famous. Apparently, Magritte painted the same theme twenty-seven times.

THREE OF FIRE

Quality: solid ideas
Planet: Sun – ego-identity, radiant Spirit, individuality

Attributes: The Three of Fire is a manifestation and an assessment. It is the outcome of an action. The Three of Fire is looking back before looking forward. It is truth and beauty. It shows integrity, positive thoughts, and goals foreseen. Opportunity, firm ideas, and the availability of the tools you need are indicated.

Advice: Look back at what you have already begun. An important part of the creative process is being able to see past patterns, showing what has worked and what hasn't.

Story: My friend, Evangel, is a dancer and choreographer. Most of her work is done solo. When she is practicing a piece for a performance, she occasionally videotapes herself so she can see how her work is progressing.

THE FIRE CHAKRA/SUIT

FOUR OF FIRE

Quality: stability
Planet: Venus – love attraction, compassion, connection

Attributes: Four of Fire is celebratory and complete. It indicates the sharing of joy and relaxing. It is being at ease with how things are developing. It is stable and confident, and indicates the external expression of success. It speaks to having a committee of support.

Advice: Your creative endeavors are on the right track. Lay a strong foundation in order to prosper.

Story: The initial ritual performed in the ceremonies of many indigenous cultures is the invocation of the four directions. In the Peruvian ceremony, Despacho, there is an intention to bring things into right alignment for the participants. It is lead by a Shaman, who invokes the four directions to claim a sacred space. This creates a temporary home, with four, elemental pillars of protection.

Participants stand or sit in a circle. Each person offers personal prayers and hopes by placing symbolic objects on an altar in the middle of circle. The objects are then wrapped up in a special package and either buried, placed in the ocean, or burned, which "dispatches" the prayers.

I am grateful to have participated in several Despachos, although it is not part of my cultural heritage.

Five, Six, Seven of Fire

Sign: Leo – Fixed Fire – bright, proud, dramatic, adventurous, charging ahead, creative
Anatomy: stomach
Touch: light or off the body

FIVE OF FIRE

Quality: amusing challenge
Planet: Saturn – order, form, disciplined, fear, contraction, transcendence

Attributes: Five of Fire strives and sustains. It is about mustering the courage to overcome obstacles. The Five of Fire is clever, forceful and strategic. It wants to release pent up energy. The Five of Fire isn't to be taken too seriously. It betokens an amusing challenge.

Advice: Lighten up and don't take your disputes so seriously. They are there to make you question and strengthen your own convictions. You are at a turning point. Learn and strategize.

Story: This card reminds me of Capoeira, the Brazilian martial art. It consists of quick movements that use leg sweeps and gymnastic-type moves. Capoeira looks like a very active dance to me. It is amusing and playful, but takes skill, timing, and spontaneity.

THE FIRE CHAKRA/SUIT

SIX OF FIRE

Quality: triumph
Planet: Jupiter – truth, faith, grace, optimistic, expansive

Attributes: Six of Fire shows a victory. It is success after working extremely hard. The Six of Fire is initiating leadership and coming out ahead. You have won.

Advice: Receiving this card acknowledges overcoming a challenge. Recognize the role of the advocacy and support of others in achieving your victory.

Story: The symbol of the Olympic games is an eternal flame. It was inspired by the Greeks and reintroduced to the Olympic games in 1928. The Olympic flame commemorates Prometheus stealing heavenly fire for humanity. In a sense, it signifies victory.

On Olympia, the flame was dedicated to Hera. Later, in classical Rome, the Vestal Virgins tended the flame. Nowadays, it is preserved by those who venerate the Goddess(es) of the hearth – Brigid, Hestia, etc.

SEVEN OF FIRE

Quality: defiant
Planet: Mars – drive, desire, courage

Attributes: Seven of Fire indicates defiance and courage. It signifies maintaining your beliefs and having the courage to follow your convictions. The Seven of Fire is powerful, righteous, and eccentric. It means setting a trend and standing up for one's own beliefs.

Advice: Follow your gut feeling. Follow what you believe in. Show defiance and take power into your own hands.

Story: De Juan grew up in the Deep South in a family of eight children. No one in his family had ever gone to college. For generations they were always farm workers.

When De Juan was in high school, he realized he had an artistic talent. De Juan sent away for college applications and forged his parent's signature on them.

When he got into art school, he surprised everyone. Off De Juan went to college. Eventually, he came back to the south and is now an art professor at the local university.

THE FIRE CHAKRA/SUIT

Eight, Nine, Ten of Fire

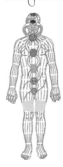

Sign: Sagittarius – Mutable Fire – big-hearted, idealistic, restless
Anatomy: thighs
Touch: deep and dispersing

EIGHT OF FIRE

Quality: outpouring passion
Planet: Mercury – reason, skill, intelligence, verbal expression

Attributes: Eight of Fire indicates moving rapidly and letting the energy flow. It is unconscious and fervent. It means releasing energy into action. The Eight of Fire is intuitive and free. It is active, swift, and unfocused.

Advice: Trust the speed at which you are going. Get out of your own way and follow the creative force. Realize your greatest passions. Spirit is moving you. Ask to be moved in an unmistakable direction.

Story: Rita is nonlinear in her action and approach to tasks. She has a lot of different commitments to fulfill and changes her mind often. What works best for her in completing her tasks is to build up energy to get things done from a flexible, unfocused approach.

When Rita was leaving her teaching job, she was confronted by the need to pack and move all her belongings into storage inside of one week. Her son was graduating from high school and, on top of everything else, the family was planning on leaving on a car trip following the move and graduation ceremonies. That entire week, Rita just kept going, somehow. Her spontaneous, diffused energy was the force behind her being able to accomplish everything on time.

NINE OF FIRE

Quality: resilient
Planet: Sun – ego-identity, radiant Spirit, individuality; and Moon – emotions, adaptable sense of self, reflective

Attributes: Nine of Fire is accomplished, successful, and often exhausting. It indicates endurance, resilience, and proven success. It is both internal and external accomplishment. The Nine of Fire indicates driven and dynamic energy.

Advice: You have emerged on the other side. You may even have a few scars or wounds to prove it. Know that it is time to wind down your efforts. Reward yourself for your labors.

Story: My client, Anita, is a real fighter. Her life isn't easy. Abuse, alcoholism, suicide, and mental illness all run in her family. She handled the life situation she was dealt begrudgingly at first, but eventually with grace. Anita is an incredibly kind person. She is always willing to help out a friend and has a deep understanding of people's idiosyncrasies. She deals with her own family and their challenges like a warrior.

THE FIRE CHAKRA/SUIT

TEN OF FIRE

Quality: over-burdened
Planet: Saturn – responsibility

Attributes: The Ten of Fire indicates an oppressive or overwhelming situation. The Ten of Fire is burdensome, difficult, and all-encompassing. A lot of passionate and creative work has been completed, but now it is weighing heavily on you.

Advice: You have been carrying the burden for far too long. You have done enough. You are enough. Contain your energy until you can stop working.

Story: Elaine is a successful contemporary painter. She always has a busy schedule and exhibition deadlines to meet. In addition to raising a family, she is incredibly prolific.

Although Elaine is very strong, one day she threw her back out while moving one of her large canvases. This resulted in her needing to have surgery. Too soon afterwards she was painting again and had to have a second surgery. It was harder for her to stop painting than it was to become a successful artist.

Fire Court Cards

SEEKS A SPIRITUAL OR CREATIVE LIFE

Art form: visual art

KING OF FIRE
Mature male – leads

Quality: vital
Sub-Element: Air

Attributes: The King of Fire indicates a passionate and courageous temperament. He is a real fighter. He has a vision. He is an inspirational, powerful leader. He is bold and confident.

His downside is that when he becomes arrogant or ego-identified he has a sharp temper.

Advice: Be inspired and have the courage to move forward. Do as Spirit moves you.

Story: Vincent Van Gogh painted so furiously that his emotions affected his work. Yet his all or nothing approach changed the history of painting forever.

THE FIRE CHAKRA/SUIT

QUEEN OF FIRE
Mature female – nurtures

Quality: transformative
Sub-Element: Water

Attributes: The Queen of Fire knows what she wants and knows how to get it. You cannot deter her. She tends to be very creative and passionate about whatever it is she's doing. She is a sexy mama. Queen of Fire can get along with everybody. She is also dedicated to her job.

On the downside, she can be single-minded and pushy.

Advice: Allow the Queen of Fire to stir up your passions and inspire whatever it is you are doing. Make sure that she doesn't bowl you over. Let her help you transform.

Story: Valerie is always creating. She moves through projects with gusto. Sometimes Valerie paints or draws or takes photographs. Other times she is writing stories, articles, or poems.

Valerie lives a creative life. She has a wide variety of friends. Coincidences are a way of life for her. She finds something magical in nature, on a city walk, or in a bookstore.

KNIGHT OF FIRE
Young adult – seeks

Quality: inspired
Sub-Element: Fire

Attributes: The Knight of Fire is confident in him or herself. S/he loves adventure. S/he tends to be daring and fearless. S/he charges ahead without warning with gust and passion.

Her/his downside is being overly zealous and can be exhausting.

Advice: Go along for the ride, just as long that you have the energy for it. This is a highly creative person and can be interested in a cause.

Story: Bhagavan Das is a 1960's counter-culture icon. Better known as Baba, he is one of the first Americans to delve into Nada Yoga teachings in India, ushering in the spiritual movement in America. He gives blessing through singing with an open heart. Baba was a mentor for Ram Das, and has sung with Bob Dylan and the Grateful Dead.

THE FIRE CHAKRA/SUIT

PAGE OF FIRE
Childlike – learns

Quality: spontaneous
Sub-Element: Earth

Attributes: The Page of Wands is focused and confident. S/he is filled with passion and has a new idea about creativity.

On the downside, s/he lacks confidence or is conceited.

Advice: Follow your Spirit and see where it leads you. Feed your creativity and inspiration.

Story: Joan of Arc was a young French peasant woman in the 15th century who claimed to be having visions and hearing voices telling her of her country's defeat. At first no one believed her and she was even tortured to test her faith in her avowals. Joan continued having visions, and kept insisting on their validity until, eventually, she led her country to victory over the English.

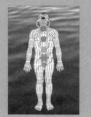

CHAPTER 9

Water Cards

THE WATER CHAKRA – "I FEEL."

The Water Chakra is also known as the Sexual or Pelvic Chakra and is located in the lower abdomen. The Sanskrit name is "Swadistana," which means "dwelling place" or "the place that has its own basis." The sound vocalization is "Vam," and the symbol is a crescent moon with six lotus petals.

As mentioned earlier, the human body is approximately 66% water; the earth's surface is most likely around 70% water. Water is the elemental medium of connecting and flowing. The Water Chakra is where the possibility of feeling emotions comes into play. The Water Chakra, or sacral center, is known to be the quintessential female source of power.

This center relates to the moon. Moon influence is adaptable and reflective. With correct, unimpeded energy flow, this Chakra can bring balance and help you find equilibrium. The Water Chakra's color is orange and it influences sexuality. Reproductive glands and gonads, testes in men and ovaries in women, are energized, maintained, and regulated under the auspices of this Chakra, and correct energy flow here can help in reproduction and development of sexual traits.

Sexual energy can be extremely powerful and, although commercialized, abused and exploited, in it can also be sacred. The Taoists believe this "sacred" energy is the source of all creativity, calling it Jing. They recognized the importance of keeping sexually active and that Jing was converted to Chi, life force.

THE WATER CHAKRA/SUIT

Keep your hands soft and relaxed. Place one hand over your forehead and one on your lower abdomen. With nurturing feelings, send a warm flowing energy throughout your body.

WATER CARDS – EMOTIONAL LIFE

Chakra: sacral
Anatomy: chest, pelvis, feet
Sense: taste
Body response: smooth and flowing
Emotions: letting go/attachment
Color: orange
Keywords: emotional, love, relationship, connect, flowing, receptive, nurturing, merging

Cups/Water cards are about emotions, relationships and human feelings. Cups/Water indicators are mainly about love relationships. They signify connecting, flowing, and nurturing. Cups/Water cards are portrayed with chalices or hearts. Cups/Water cards are often about the relationship of mother to child, lovers, or individually, about connecting our feet to the ground.

Cups/Water cards may also indicate the occult or addictions. They signify the quest or search for the Universal or the Divine. Cups/Water influence the need of boundaries. They also indicate flow. Cups/Water need a container to hold, encompass, and form emotional and energetic content, as Water Element is a liquid quality.

ACE OF WATER

Quality: new emotions
Signs: all Water signs – Cancer, Scorpio, Pisces
Anatomy: all Water anatomy – chest, pelvis and feet

Attributes: Ace of Water is the source of everything psychic. It is a new way of feeling. The Ace of Water is good health, joy and love. It is the potential for any kind of love – friendly, maternal or romantic. The cup, chalice, nurturing cauldron-of-plenty, or heart shapes are common symbols for the watery emotions and love.

Advice: You are at the beginning of a new love. Go with the flow. Stay calm and connected to your feelings. The love you are feeling can heal you.

Story: When my niece was born, I remember speaking to my brother, who was so excited. He said, "I'm in love!" He went on to explain that this wasn't like falling in love romantically, but was something else entirely.

My niece is now grown, but she still loves her papa and her papa loves her. There's a mutual admiration that started from the day of her birth.

THE WATER CHAKRA/SUIT

Two, Three, Four of Water

Sign: Cancer – Cardinal Water – compassionate, sensitive, nurturing, protective
Anatomy: chest, breast
Touch: rocking

TWO OF WATER

Quality: union of opposites
Planet: Venus – love, attraction, compassion, connection

Attributes: Two of Water signifies love. It indicates opening the heart to another person or even to a thing. It is a union of opposites or likes and signals the impulse to reach out. It is the beginning of a romance, or a friendship, or a mother to child connection. It is refreshing, attractive and intimate. The Two of Water is the potential to merge with another.

Advice: Appreciate the love that has come your way. Who or what are you connecting to? Feel your heart expand. Learn about love. Stay present in what you are feeling. Let those feelings flow. Learn about love and how it can heal the heart.

Story: For several years on a regular basis on every new moon and full moon, I have been exchanging Tarot card readings with my neighbor, Jenny. When I was single, I would pick Two of Water as something I desired in almost every reading. I would pull this card even when I was not consciously thinking about wanting to be in a relationship. It became a joke.

Now that I am in an established relationship, this card never shows up.

THREE OF WATER

Quality: celebration
Planet: Mercury – reason, skill, intelligence, verbal expression

Attributes: Three of Water is playful. It is expressive, rejoicing, and loving. The Three of Water communicates and celebrates with friends.

Advice: Oh, just go and have some fun. Bring along your friends. Play, enjoy and feel the gratitude. Dance like you have never danced before.

Story: After I moved to New York City, right after college, I would periodically meet with three of my childhood girlfriends. We would share a meal and sometimes dance freely in our living rooms or outside on the streets. It was always so much fun, and a relief from the challenges we faced in New York. We would tell jokes, laugh until our stomachs ached. Our visits always felt so magical and empowering. They brought us to a place of celebration and contentment.

THE WATER CHAKRA/SUIT

FOUR OF WATER

Quality: stagnation
Planet: Moon – emotions, adaptable sense of self, reflective

Attributes: Four of Water is still, stable, and safe. At times it is comfortable, even luxurious. Other times it is stagnant and apathetic.

Advice: Calming down your emotions could be the safe way to go, or it could be like building a moat around your emotions. Make sure you are safe but not detached from your feelings. Wait until a proper flow begins to happen before moving forward.

Story: My last year of teaching in the private school in New York was the worst. I should've left sooner, but I didn't know where to go. Two schools had merged and I was teaching a difficult class schedule. I was teaching a wide range of ages, which made planning a challenge. I stopped liking my students and I found the administration lacking a moral core. I ceased caring after years of loving teaching art. I was stuck. I was just trying to get through the year. Lucky for me, this was my last year teaching in that capacity. Very close to the end of the school year, I found out I was one of many who were being laid off.

Five, Six, Seven of Water

Sign: Scorpio – Fixed Water – passionate, deep, fearless
Anatomy: pelvis
Touch: light or off the body

FIVE OF WATER

Quality: disappointment
Planet: Mars – drive, desire, courage

Attributes: Five of Water is disappointing, lonely, and difficult. It shows extreme emotional loss and disillusionment. It is about feeling alone and yet the loss indicates the need to let go. It is a turn in the road and provides hope.

Advice: Failing is easier if you can accept that it is part of growing and changing. It is the anticipation of failing that is difficult. It is time to move on. Nothing was ever created without mistakes. Find the courage to continue. Repeat: *Find the courage to continue.* There is always hope.

Story: While living in New York City, I started dating Gordon, one of my closest friends. Although warned by a mutual friend that he had difficulty in relationships, I thought I had fallen in love. This was going to be different.

When Gordon dumped me eight months later, I was devastated. His accusations seemed unjust. It was also such bad timing for me. I resented him and his therapist. We could not maintain a friendship anymore. I shamed myself for not listening to our friend or living up to some standard that turned out to be an illusion.

THE WATER CHAKRA/SUIT

SIX OF WATER

Quality: reciprocity
Planet: Sun – ego-identity, radiant Spirit, individuality

Attributes: Six of Water is friendly, generous, and kind. It is giving out of love. Six of Water is pleasure and charity. It is a mutual exchange.

Advice: Be grateful for having an open heart. Do not consciously give just to get something back. Reciprocity means that everything will come back.

Story: For years Sheila taught high school English in a very poor community. Most of her students rarely got to go far from home. So Sheila brought different cultures to them to experience. Every year she would create a replica of a proper English Tea that took weeks of preparation. Some of her students didn't even know what a saucer was. The experience was always a great success. Now that Sheila is retired, she and her friends have proper teas on a regular basis, rotating the host. The teas have become an important part of sharing a social life.

SEVEN OF WATER

Quality: fantasies
Planet: Venus – love, attraction, compassion, connection

Attributes: Seven of Water indicates over extended emotional states. This is a card that has evolved for me over the years, sometimes embracing opposite meanings. The Seven of Water could indicate self-indulgence to the point of debauchery. Or, on the other hand, it can indicate harmless fantasies, filled with hope, that help us to dream big for the sake of obtaining higher goals.

Advice: Take hold of your desires. Reach for what you want. Use fantasy and dreaming as a vehicle for reaching for something better. Recognize that your fantasies are fantasies, and can be employed to create what you want. Ask for the best and most for yourself.

Story: Donald is married with two children. He works as a financial planner and his wife is a real estate agent. They love each other and are committed to their children. In his spare time, Donald practices martial arts. His dream is to own his own dojo, a martial arts studio. Although he may never reach this dream, it keeps him going.

Whenever he gets frustrated, he uses his fantasy to ease the tension. It helps make his busy schedule a lot easier to deal with. Plus, this practice of focusing on his dream promises that it is that much more likely to manifest in his life in a positive way.

THE WATER CHAKRA/SUIT

Sign: Pisces – Mutable Water – romantic, idealistic, compassionate
Anatomy: feet
Touch: deep and dispersing

EIGHT OF WATER

Quality: change
Planet: Saturn – order, form, disciplined, fear, contraction, transcendence

Attributes: The Eight of Water indicates abandonment and indolence. It is taking the Path of Least Resistance in a tired, or no longer viable, situation. The card gives us the ability to walk away from any circumstances, especially if they are emotionally charged. It indicates setting boundaries. The Eight of Water makes choices by departing and/or making a separation.

Advice: Get out of your own way. Find a way to walk away from emotionally charged situations. This is not giving up. It is giving a situation some space.

Story: The Albany Bulb, in the East of San Francisco, reminds me of the Eight of Water. It is a landfill peninsula created by a collection of large freeway sections that collapsed during the earthquake. Nature has taken over. The Bulb has become an unsupervised walkway between the Bay and the freeway. New sculptures can often be found there. If you look long enough you can see campsites of homeless people hidden in the brush.

The Bulb is also a dog walk and a place for anyone who needs a quick getaway, without the commitment of going up into the hills. I have often walked the Bulb when I needed some time and space.

NINE OF WATER

Quality: completion
Planet: Jupiter – truth, faith, grace, optimistic, expansive

Attributes: Nine of Water betokens gratifying, fulfilled dreams and complete pleasure. The card affirms satisfaction. The Nine of Water is about being physically and emotionally healthy.

Advice: Take ownership of what you want. Observe what will make you happy. Look around and see what you've created. Pat yourself on the back. You are past the difficulties and now allow yourself to reap the benefits. Experience being grateful. Gratitude is giving back to Spirit. It is what many religions are based on. Find what drives you.

Story: Katherine is very psychic and has a strong personality. For a long time she questioned why she had trouble finding a mate. She certainly had a lot of friends. This was frustrating to Katherine. I could see it in her body. She would ask the Tarot how to change this particular situation in every possible way.

When Katherine finally stopped trying, she found a partner. He was not what she expected, and yet her whole demeanor changed. Katherine's partner is not intimidated by her powerful presence.

THE WATER CHAKRA/SUIT

TEN OF WATER

Quality: Abundance
Planet: Mars – drive, desire, courage

Attributes: Ten of Water signifies contentment in a family or group setting. It means sharing joy with others. It is a celebration of accomplishments – blissful and complete. At times it may become boring and feel overindulged. What is next?

Advice: Enjoy your family bliss. Appreciate the over flow and let it run through you like a waterfall. You are home. What really makes you happy? What makes you feel comfortable?

Story: Throughout the '80s I shared a summer rental with friends in a huge and funky mansion in upstate New York designed after a Mediterranean home, named Villa Nanté. On any given weekend evening, after a day of gallivanting around the countryside, we would share a meal at the long table in the dining room, the walls of which were covered with faded carpets. It was a room from another era.

We'd all have a separate dish to prepare in a kitchen that belonged to no one person. We could all enjoy cooking together, which often made our meals resemble a banquet. Villa Nanté was a welcome respite to our hectic weekday lives in the City.

Water Court Cards

SEEKS AN EMOTIONAL LIFE

Art form: cooking

KING OF WATER
Mature male – leads

Quality: loyal
Sub-Element: Air

Attributes: The King of Water is a benevolent leader. He is aware of his own feelings and considers the feelings of others before making a decision. He has an open heart and is wise. He accepts people for who they are. He has a mature and committed approach to his relationships.

On the downside, he may become cruel, heartless and dishonorable.

Advice: Accept the love this person has to offer. He is in control of his emotions. Let him guide you, through his open heart.

Story: Poppy Bernie, my mother's father, was the kindest, warmest grandfather anyone could ever have. Everybody loved him. I loved visiting him in Florida, where he had retired with my grandmother. We got to go swimming and lie out in the sun all day. At night we took turns sitting on his lap. I still remember his laugh, and the smell of his cigars. He was so generous and friendly to everybody. When he died even the woman in the insurance office cried.

THE WATER CHAKRA/SUIT

QUEEN OF WATER
Mature female – nurtures

Quality: integrity
Sub-Element: Water

Attributes: The Queen of Water focuses on her emotionality. She is very loving and understanding and is willing to help anyone. She is extremely intuitive. She is self-aware, very supportive and accepts whatever you do. The Queen of Water is warm and affectionate due to her tender heart. She is empathetic and sympathetic.

On the downside she can be overbearing and worrisome.

Advice: Accept the love from the people in your life. Be warm and kind. Accept your intuitive abilities to come through any situation.

Story: One of the most beloved Buddhist deities is Quan Yin, the goddess of compassion. Statues of her depict a slender woman with long flowing robes, carrying a lotus flower. Quan Yin is popular throughout China, India, and now North America. I find it a comforting reminder of her love and grace whenever I see her statue.

KNIGHT OF WATER
Young adult – seeks

Quality: desire
Sub-Element: Fire

Attributes: The Knight of Water tends to be forceful in quiet way. S/he is the great romantic, and dashes off to rescue people in need or distress. S/he may even gush and be sentimental and over-sensitive. The Knight of Water is warm and giving. This card indicates the pursuit of love relationships.

Her/His downside is that s/he wears her/his heart on his/her sleeve, and might be inclined to seduce anyone.

Advice: If you are looking for romance, this is the person for you. S/he opens you up to sharing, and to creatively fantasizing.

Story: In the 1990 film *Pretty Woman*, written by J.F. Lawton and directed by Garry Marshall, Edward, a wealthy businessman, hires Vivian as an escort. Although Vivian is smart and beautiful, she has had to resort to prostitution. Edward is a callous businessman. Over their time together, Vivian and Edward both soften and fall in love. Edward is Vivian's Knight of Water.

THE WATER CHAKRA/SUIT

PAGE OF WATER
Childlike – learns

Chakra: Water – sacral
Sub-Element: Earth

Attributes: The Page of Water has a very youthful energy. S/he may represent the beginning of a romance. S/he is flirtatious and affectionate. S/he is an idealistic. The Page of Water is filled with expectations of love and intimacy.

On the downside s/he is hypersensitive and delusional.

Advice: Ask who is the romantic, visionary person in your life right now? Is it you? Who are you falling in love with? What is coming into your life that you are in love with?

Story: I met Jason when he and his mom moved into the upstairs apartment, and he was attending high school. Jason was a romantic dreamer. Ever since I first met him he's had these idealistic views of changing the world. I remember when Jason's first girlfriend broke up with him and how upset he felt.

Now that Jason is in college, I still keep tabs on him through his mom. He still has ideals, although he is majoring in science. I was glad to hear that he had a new girlfriend and was dancing with a dance company. He still has big dreams.

CHAPTER 10

Earth Cards

EARTH CHAKRA – "I AM."

Known as the Root or Earth Chakra, this Chakra is located at the base of the spine and relates to the perineum, the space below the pelvic floor and in front of the anus. The name in Sanskrit is "Muladhara," meaning "root support." The Earth Chakra supplies our physical, energetic, and spiritual support and grounding. It influences the issues of money and career. The Earth Chakra helps us to focus and feel like we belong. The color is red and the Sanskrit symbol is a square with four crimson petals for grounding and root support. Support from proper flow and functioning of the Earth Chakra is vital to all functions of the body, emotions, mind, and Spirit. It is from the Earth/Root Chakra that the coiled serpent of Kundalini energy rises to vitalize and illuminate the entire organism of Self.

The divine consciousness of Deva, the Creator, is associated with this center.

Earth is practical and substantial and the planetary influence of Saturn supplies order, form and transcendence. The adrenal glands are associated with the Earth Chakra, supporting and regulating blood pressure, heart rate, and energy levels in the body. The sound vocalization is "Lam," and the symbols that corresponds to the Earth Chakra are the square or cube.

EARTH CHAKRA/SUIT – SELF-SOOTHER

Keep your hands soft yet solid. Place one hand on the back of the neck, holding gently, and one on the base of your spine. Feel your feet solidly on the ground. Project a feeling of earthly security and safety.

THE EARTH CHAKRA/SUIT

Earth Cards - physical life

Chakra: root
Anatomy: neck, colon, knees
Sense: smell
Body response: contraction
Emotions: courage/fear
Color: deep red
Keywords: physical, sense, work, money, structure, methodical, organized, grounded

Earth/Pentacle cards are everything physical or literal. They are about work, money issues and structure. They put everything into practical perspective. Earth/Pentacle cards point out our physical needs. The suit of Earth/Pentacle is also known equally known as Disks or Coins. A five star pattern often appears on these cards, symbolizing the human body.

ACE OF EARTH

Quality: beginning
Signs: all Earth signs – Taurus, Virgo, Capricorn
Anatomy: all Earth anatomy – neck, colon, knees

Attributes: Ace of Earth is a beginning of something tangible, a new enterprise, or a new way of receiving money. You may be starting a new job. There is a literal shift of some kind. A seed has been planted.

Advice: Nurture the project you have already begun developing. Give it the right amount of light, space, and love. If you have a new source of money, do not squander or hoard it. Be wise, slow, and methodical. Don't neglect or sabotage your strong foundation.

Story: Last spring, I helped my friend plant some very sturdy-looking starter plants, which had just germinated from seeds, in a rocky, untilled garden. I followed his instructions and stuck them in the earth between rocks and chunks of dirt. I was skeptical of these conditions, but after I mulched and watered the garden well, the starters grew rapidly into healthy and delicious vegetables.

THE EARTH CHAKRA/SUIT

Two, Three, Four of Earth

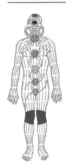

Sign: Capricorn – Cardinal Earth – solid, cautious, structured, self-controlled
Anatomy: knees
Touch: rocking

TWO OF EARTH

Quality: balance
Planet: Jupiter – truth, faith, grace, optimistic, expansive

Attributes: Two of Earth is harmony and change. It is juggling two things at once. Two of Earth is partnerships or duality. It is yin and yang or balance.

Advice: Find the appropriate balance in whatever you are doing.

Story: I have a twin brother. We both live in the SF Bay Area. In some ways we are so different. And in others ways we are so much alike. I'm conscious of my body. He's not. I speak slowly; he speaks fast. We are similar in that we both like, and try to help, other people. We are also both feminists.

Although we are now in different career fields, I used to silkscreen in a find arts studio and he still has a silkscreen T-shirt business. Whenever anyone comments on us being twins, they either say we're so much alike or we're so different. We agree with whatever they say. We're kind of like yin and yang.

THREE OF EARTH

Quality: negotiating
Planet: Mars – drive, desire, courage

Attributes: Three of Earth indicates a group activity. It often refers to negotiating a business deal or a way of working together. Three of Earth portends the synthesizing of ideas into successful efforts. It suggests being one part of a triad or apprentice training.

Advice: Respect and work with others around you. Everybody involved has a role. Everyone is connected. Harmonize all factors in order to create.

Story: In my twenties I worked for a non-profit silkscreen studio. One of my jobs was to set up other groups to print their own posters. I would narrow down the printing variables, set up the registration, get the inks mixed according to the type of paper, image details, and screen mesh.

Even though each person was given a specific task, they all had to watch and make sure nothing was going wrong, which could cause hours of delay. The more smoothly things went, the faster and easier it was to get successful posters.

THE EARTH CHAKRA/SUIT

FOUR OF EARTH

Quality: stability
Planet: Sun – ego-identity, radiant Spirit, individuality

Attributes: Four of Earth indicates a structure, powerful and whole. It is stable and focused. Four of Earth indicates protectiveness. Sometimes Four of Earth means holding onto one's self so tightly it comes across as selfish.

Advice: Learn the right use of power. Observe your boundaries and refrain from crossing into inappropriate actions. Find your stability and let go.

Story: One of my main intentions in my bodywork practice and my card readings is to empower my clients. In both practices, I acknowledge what is and then help them to feel grounded enough to meet their challenges.

Henry has a degenerative disease that affects his muscles. I am never going to make his condition go away. What I can do is help Henry get into a relaxed enough state where he feels positive about what he can do, and be patient with what he cannot.

Five, Six, Seven of Earth

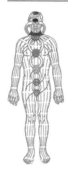

Sign: Taurus – Fixed Earth – secure, stubborn, slow, possessive, strong, loving comfort, beauty
Anatomy: neck
Touch: light or off the body

FIVE OF EARTH

Quality: concerns
Planet: Mars – drive, desire, courage

Attributes: Five of Earth informs us there is a conflict, worry, or concern. The card tells us of a difficult situation. Five of Earth suggests a lonely and hurtful feeling and/or an idea that one doesn't have enough resources. This thought may be conscious or not. The Five of Earth may also indicate actual health issues or perhaps being a hypochondriac.

Advice: Stop feeling sorry for yourself. Do not try and escape suffering or compare yourself to others. Difficult situations are easier to deal with if you can be in the present.

Story: After graduating art school, I worked all sorts of freelance art related jobs. One chilly December, there wasn't much work and I had very little savings left in my bank account. I was depressed and worried, especially with all the impending holiday season expenses looming. I wasn't sure how I was going to pay my next month's rent, much less participate in extravagant "high-holiday" festivities, but I stayed calm and centered.

Out of nowhere a friend referred an interior designer to me, who needed to purchase artwork for several model apartments he was designing. The designer came over to my loft and bought about twelve pieces of art. I sold them cheaply but what I had made got me out of my depression and discomfort.

THE EARTH CHAKRA/SUIT

SIX OF EARTH

Quality: generosity, triumph
Planet: Moon – emotions, adaptable sense of self, reflective

Attributes: The Six of Earth shows the qualities of being generous and responsive. It tells us to be generous in our giving. The Six of Earth can be either a benefactor or a beneficiary. It indicates helping others without concern about getting something back. The Six of Earth connects and uplifts us. It is sometimes about needing more money.

Advice: You may be compelled towards generosity for no particular reason. You may receive a gift that you don't expect. Allow and appreciate that your gifts will be valued. In many religions, giving assures a place in heaven. I think good actions will determine the future.

Story: My sister Judy has been donating blood for years. She has given over fifty gallons of blood. Judy never knows where her blood goes. She just does it. When people ask her how she does it, she says, "One pint at a time."

SEVEN OF EARTH

Quality: inner work
Planet: Saturn – order, form, disciplined, fear, contraction, transcendence

Attributes: Seven of Earth is either patient or impatient. The card is about waiting for things to grow and change, or fears of failing. Seven of Earth reminds us to let things take their course. It sets limits.

Advice: If you resist timely progression and processing you will fail. Wait. Be brave and stick with it. Patience is a virtue. Your pursuits will be completed. A lesson in patience is trusting something is going to happen, even if it takes time.

Story: I have been impatient my whole life. This comes from what I learned as a child. I do not like having to wait because I might get bored or lose momentum.

I was recommended to give short Polarity Therapy treatments to a group of hard working production managers in an ad agency, with the intent to improve communication. I was ready to get started as soon as I heard of the possibility. Because of timing and corporate procedures there were long intervals between approvals and setting up the program. It took three months from my initial contact before I actually started working on the premises. There were so many times in those months that I was ready to give up on the possibility of working there. In hindsight, I understood that the timing was perfect.

THE EARTH CHAKRA/SUIT

Eight, Nine, Ten of Earth

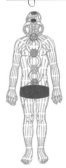

Sign: Virgo – Mutable Earth – meticulous, orderly, servile
Anatomy: colon
Touch: deep and dispersing

EIGHT OF EARTH

Quality: change and inspiration
Planet: Sun – ego, identity, radiant Spirit, individuality

Attributes: The Eight of Earth card tells us about developing a skill or trade. It announces hard, meticulous work and the benefits to come. The Eight of Earth is so involved in working that you lose track of time. Perseverance equals and leads to success. It is sustained and focused.

Advice: Keep moving forward. Focus on what you are doing and let distractions fall away. Create a ritual or visualization around accomplishing your goals before you begin to work. Repeat the rewards of your labors.

Story: When I do bodywork, I am always surprised by how fast or slowly the session goes by. Things happen *IN* time, not *ON* time. What seems to be an hour can really be a few hours. When this happens, it is usually because I am fully immersed in what I am doing.

There are times when I am working where I cannot seem to get anything done and the hours tick away. Other times it seems I get a lot done in a short amount of time.

NINE OF EARTH

Quality: completion
Planet: Venus – love, attraction, compassion, connection

Attributes: The Nine of Earth signals happiness and satisfaction. It means reaching our full potential, being content and confident. The Nine of Earth represents joy in the flow.

Advice: Relax and enjoy. Notice what satisfaction feels like. Share your bountiful blessings.

Story: After I teach weekend trainings, I feel completely satisfied. Being paid a chunk of money is nice but, mostly, I enjoy sharing information and experience, knowing others will benefit. Several years ago, I had this teaching gig in Salt Lake City, to go once a month for ten consecutive months to teach practitioners in Polarity Therapy.

I had my routine down and would often stay a few extra days to give sessions. I got to appreciate students other than Californians or New Yorkers. I loved sharing my knowledge with people who were hungry for learning comprehensive energy work.

I would come home every month and relish in my contentment. On those trips I was the Queen Healer.

THE EARTH CHAKRA/SUIT

TEN OF EARTH

Quality: abundance
Planet: Mercury – reason, skill, intelligence, verbal expression

Attributes: The Ten of Earth is completion. It usually refers to financial wealth and prosperity. The Ten of Earth tells us about sharing and rejoicing with family. It indicates the ultimate of material comforts.

Advice: Your self-esteem is at an all-time high. Enjoy and share with others.

Story: After Jenny's two children had grown, she and her husband got divorced. Jenny decided to focus on what she really wanted to do, which was to play music and continue to develop her meditation practice. She rented out the main part of her house to her beloved niece's young family. She fixed up the back cottage as a music studio. When she was raising her children this wasn't an option. It was always her husband who was considered the musician.

Now Jenny meditates regularly and teaches piano in the afternoons. Her yard looks great, she has plenty of friends, and her niece's family is her family. Best of all, Jenny plays music in a band and writes her own songs. All of this took several years.

Recently, after a long day and after meditating, Jenny had a physical experience of complete bliss and wellbeing. I think she had a peak experience as described by Maslow, and which corresponds to the Crown Chakra consciousness of liberation from the self-limiting ego.

Earth Court Cards

SEEKS A PHYSICAL LIFE

Art form: sculpture, aromatherapy

KING OF EARTH

Mature male – leads

Quality: prosperous
Sub-Element: Air

Attributes: The King of Earth is practical and confident. He is someone who will assess a situation and takes control calmly. He is very reliable and is a good business and financial leader. He is authoritative and stable.

On the downside, he can be arrogant and miserly.

Advice: Trust the leadership capabilities that are at hand. They are strong and solid. If it is a money issue you are asking about, follow through.

Story: The Charles Dickens story, *A Christmas Carol*, tells the tale of Ebenezer Scrooge, a wealthy but stingy and nasty man, who is transformed by visits from the Spirits of Christmases past, present, and future. After the visits, he becomes generous and joyful, especially towards his employee, whose family is poor and has a crippled child.[1]

THE EARTH CHAKRA/SUIT

QUEEN OF EARTH
Mature female – nurtures

Quality: health conscious
Sub-Element: Water

Attributes: The Queen of Earth is the quintessential Earth Mother. She gives us a sense of security and connectedness. She is interested in community. The Queen of Earth loves being at home and has a practical realistic view of life. She is very kind and nurturing. Her greatest desire is to take physical care of others.

On the downside she can manifest as sluggish and stagnant.

Advice: Trust this person and let them into your life.

Story: Georgia owns a car repair shop. It is an unusual vocation for a woman over seventy, but she is successful. Her shop is the hippest place in town, if a car repair shop can be hip. The office is actually pleasant, and several times a month the garage gets cleared of cars to host community events.

Georgia is also a marvelous homemaker. She loves to entertain and cook huge meals for her family and friends.

KNIGHT OF EARTH
Young adult – seeks

Quality: builder, athlete
Sub-Element: Fire

Attributes: The Knight of Earth tends to be calm and complacent. Even though he is interested in accomplishing a task, he moves forward slowly and methodically. The Knight of Earth is practical and organized. He can help you move ahead in any project.

On the downside, he can be smug.

Advice: Learn to be patient. This person and/or influence can help you get things done without burning out.

Story: Philip Johnson was one of the most well-known and prolific postmodern architects. He built huge corporate buildings throughout the country. His designs are very contemporary but have classical components. I remember when his *ATandT* building first went up in NYC. It changed the whole skyline. I wondered what compelled him.

THE EARTH CHAKRA/SUIT

PAGE OF EARTH

Quality: precocious
Sub-Element: Earth

Attributes: Page of Earth is practical. S/he is a studious and contemplative. S/he is a reliable and grounded worker. S/he is also good at planning and committed to learning.

On the downside s/he is a "know it all."

Advice: Learn how to learn.

Story: St. Matthew, one of the twelve apostles who followed Jesus in the New Testament, was known to be a tax collector. He was also literate and is usually pictured reading or studying, which was unusual for his time.

Crystals and gemstones are tools for enhancing energy and spiritual growth. They are a source of healing and magic that have been used for centuries.

The most common use of crystals and gemstones is as jewelry. Jewelry protects and adorns. I once heard a jewelry historian say, "Never trust a woman who doesn't wear jewelry." In her mind, there was a deep feminine quality missing in a woman who did not desire to beautify herself.

Crystals were placed on Egyptian Tombs. In China, crystals and gemstones were associated with the realms of the gods. In India, ornamental gemstones aided in health issues and were designed so the stone could touch the skin. Crystals also feature in world mythologies.

Besides following the numerous books on the market and websites, a great way to find how a crystal or gemstone affects us is to follow our intuition. Hold a stone in your hands and see what comes to you. Some stones work well for some people and not for others. You have to experiment. In this section, let the Chakra distinctions for the cards point you in the right direction as to what stone to use. There are no rights or wrongs – at worst, I've seen crystals keep someone awake.

In the 1980s, while I was living in New York, crystals became very popular. Vendors were selling crystals and gemstones on street corners. My friends and I became interested in incorporating crystals into healing work. We tried placing them under our pillows at night and in our pockets. We experimented with placing them on our Chakras, and making star patterns around each other's bodies. We would then observe what happened.

One day, I was wearing a clear quartz crystal on a chain around my neck when I went to visit friends in the suburbs who had a three year old. Grace was sitting across on my lap facing me and looking at the crystal. She asked me what it was. I told her that it was a crystal and I held the crystal up and I pointed it at her. I thought, "Make Grace laugh." She smiled and chuckled a little and then said to me, "Do it to Mommy." I never said a word.

Crystals are the perfect adjunct to make a Tarot card reading a healing. After giving a reading, leave your cards out and place crystals on top of them to encourage the issue or dispel the energy.

USING CRYSTALS AND GEMSTONES WITH THE TAROT

I advise you to clean your crystals before you use them. I suggest either burying them in your backyard or placing them out in the sun. They can also be left out overnight in a window that the moonlight reaches. My favorite way of cleaning crystals and gemstones is placing them in a bowl of saltwater in the light of the full moon.

Here is a general framework. I've grouped them by Chakra/Suit. Suggested crystals for the Aces are all a variety of quartz, representing purity. The rest of the Minor Arcana is divided up in threes, into their astrological signifiers. The Major Arcana crystal and gemstone correspondences are culled from numerous sources, listed in the bibliography, and of course are mainly guided by my intuition.

These correspondences and definitions are not exclusive. Each crystal can have several meanings and it is up to you whether to balance or counterbalance the energy of any given card. "Balancing energy" in this context entails encouraging the meaning of the card. Counterbalancing is when you are clearing or intentionally changing the card meaning. Focus on what it is you want, and tell the crystal.

Guide to Tarot, Crystals, and Gemstones Correspondences

MAJOR ARCANA

Fool 0
Aventurine will support good luck and fortune.

Major Arcana Cards I–VII: Ether Chakra
Rubies help support loyalty.
Use **emeralds** for eternal joy.
Fresh water **pearls** focus attention.

Major Arcana Cards VIII–XIV: Third eye Chakra
Opals are for love and passion.
Moonstones balance the feminine with the masculine.
Turquoise is about magic and wisdom.

Major Arcana Cards XV–XXI: Crown Chakra
Diamonds purify.
Amethyst will heal on all levels.
Sapphires are for beauty and love.
Onyx helps continue your vision and add insight.
Azurite enhances a connection to the divine.

Minor Arcana

AIR CHAKRA CARDS

Ace of Air ···

Brazilian quartz crystals sends energy and amplifies.

Two, Three, Four of Air ···

Blue Tourmaline brings mental peace.

Five, Six, Seven of Air ··

Amazonite improves thinking.

Eight, Nine, Ten of Air ···

Fluorite transforms negativity.

Air Court Cards ···

Sodalite will bring out the true communications.

FIRE CHAKRA CARDS

Ace of Fire ··

Rutilated (mineral infused) **quartz** crystals for focus.

Two, Three, Four of Fire ···

Tiger Eye is for good luck.

Five, Six, Seven of Fire ···

Geodes help in seeing the whole picture.

Eight, Nine, Ten of Fire ··

Carnelian clears confusion.

Fire Court Cards ··

Aquamarine improves insight.

USING CRYSTALS AND GEMSTONES WITH THE TAROT

Ace of Water ···

Rose quartz is for love.

Two, Three, Four of Water ···

Cowrie Shells help with establishing new relationships.

Five, Six, Seven of Water ···

Pearls reduce stress and balance emotions.

Eight, Nine, Ten of Water ···

Aquamarine cleanses anything that is stagnant.

Water Court Cards ···

Sapphires are for beauty and love.

EARTH CHAKRA CARDS

Ace of Earth ···

Smoky quartz grounds and cleanses.

Two, Three, Four of Earth ··

Jade is for positive abundance.

Five, Six, Seven of Earth ···

Emeralds are for eternal joy.

Eight, Nine, Ten of Earth ···

Aventurine is for financial good luck.

Earth Court Cards ··

Bloodstone is to invoke strength.

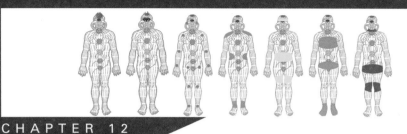

Bodywork

There are many ways of helping someone else change and heal. A bodywork session gives this structure.

Bodywork is more than Massage Therapy. Massage is about doing in a tactile way, and although it has a great range within itself, bodywork also includes other manipulative therapies, point work, and energy work. Several of the energy based therapies emphasize being and not doing.

There are over eighty types of bodywork modalities practiced in California alone.
Any card or set of cards chosen that either present a challenge or a possible desire to enhance indicates a place to start lining up someone else's Chakras or do hands-on body work.

Do not do this for someone else unless you have permission.

BASIC BODYWORK MOVES

After doing a reading for someone else, leave the cards out on a near by table. Choose a challenge card or a card or suit that is predominate or that stands out.
Find the Chakra(s) that those cards attribute.

Have your client lie down facing upward.

Place your hands about 2–4 inches above that Chakra. Visualize that Chakra(s) spinning. Move down or up the body, lining the Chakras up and connecting them with color cords, similar to the individual Chakra meditations.

If there are two Chakra/Suits that you'd like to work with, place one hand over each Chakra. Try and connect those two, even if they are not next to each other.

TAROT & BODYWORK, PRACTICE & FOODS

WHAT IS YOUR CLIENT'S EXPERIENCE?
WHAT IS YOUR EXPERIENCE?
DO THEY CORRESPOND TO THE CARDS?

I've assigned each Chakra/Suit certain subtle moves reflected in Polarity Therapy elemental protocols, along with a specific recommended bodywork modality. Try experiencing different types of bodywork. Remember: resonating with a specific trained practitioner is the most important.

WHAT ARE THE ELEMENTAL QUALITIES OF YOUR
PREFERRED BODYWORK MODALITY AND PRACTITIONER?
DOES IT CHANGE OVER TIME?
DOES IT MATCH OR OPPOSE YOUR TAROT CARD READINGS?

Crown Chakra/Suit

SUBTLE MOVES

Facing the head of the client lying on their back, and gently coming from the sides of the head, slowly place your hands under the client's head, cupping your hands as a cradle. Listen with your hands to the subtle pulses in the entire body.

Go to the feet of your client. With your thumbs and index fingers, hold the tips of each Ether toe. Gently pull.

SPECIFIC MODALITY

Cranio-Sacral Therapy is a light touch modality, which adjusts the fine flow of cerebrospinal fluid through out the spinal column. It works with the central nervous system by aligning the bones and membranes in the skull. Results are profound.

TAROT & BODYWORK, PRACTICE & FOODS

Third Eye Chakra/Suit

SUBTLE MOVES

Face the head of the client lying on their back.

Place one hand on the top of the forehead and one holding under the base of the skull.

Gently give your client a little traction.

Go to the feet of your client. Move your hands to cup under your client's heels. Hold and pull gently towards your own body.

SPECIFIC MODALITY

Reiki is a system that originated in Japan in the late 1800s that consists of transmitting universal life force. Reiki is simple and pure.

As alternative healing becomes more and more popular in the western world, Reiki has become in demand. The main premise behind Reiki is to relax and feel love. It always begins with a clear intention.

Ether Chakra/Suit

SUBTLE MOVES

Start with a head cradle.

Go down the right side of the body and place, with hands contacting the joints with a light touch, one hand on the shoulder and one hand on the wrist.

Hold and wait for the unifying pulse.

Wrist and ankle: Hold and wait for the unifying pulse

Hip and foot: Hold and wait for the unifying pulse.

Now, contact both feet. Hold and wait for the unifying pulse.

Repeat going up the left side of the body, foot and hip.

Ankle and wrist: Hold and wait for the unifying pulse.

Wrist and shoulder: Hold and wait for the unifying pulse.

Return to the top of the body and repeat the head cradle.

SPECIFIC MODALITY

Polarity Therapy is a profound holistic health care system that balances life energy in the body. It is based on the concept that we are fields of vibrating energy.

It includes bodywork, cleansing and health building diets, simple exercises, and communication skills. Polarity brings about presence and intention. It is a container to include many other bodywork modalities. Polarity Therapy is mentioned throughout this book. It is suggested for balancing of any kind.

TAROT & BODYWORK, PRACTICE & FOODS

Air Chakra/Suit

SUBTLE MOVES

With the client lying on the back, start with a head cradle.

Going down the right side of the body, touch the right shoulder with your left hand, and underneath the body, touch above the side of the waist (right kidney) with your right hand. Hold and wait for the unifying pulse.

Now move your left hand to touch where your right hand was (right kidney), and your right hand to the right ankle. Hold and wait for the unifying pulse.

Move to contacting both ankles. Hold and wait for the unifying pulse.

Hold each Air toe. Hold and wait for the unifying pulse. [See chart on page 202.]

Repeat moves going up the left side of the body.

Place the left hand to left ankle and right hand to left kidney. Hold and wait for the unifying pulse.

Place the left hand to right kidney and right hand to left shoulder. Hold and wait for the unifying pulse.

Return to the top of the body and repeat the head cradle.

SPECIFIC MODALITY

Rosen Method works to reduce stress by gentle direct touch to the body primarily on the back. Rosen Method focuses on relieving muscle tension and shifts in the breath. Developed by Marion Rosen (1914– 2012) a German immigrant, the technique is taught through osmosis. The work connects the heart to the soul.

I had the good fortune to hear Marion Rosen speak at an open house a few years before she died. Marion was already in her 80s and continued to teach and do her work. She had a presence, calmness, and charm about her that has stayed with me to this day. I often think I want to be like Marion when I am in my eighties.

Fire Chakra/Suit

SUBTLE MOVES

With the client lying on the back, start with a head cradle.

Going down the right side of the body, place your left hand just above the forehead and your right hand on the abdomen. Hold and wait for the unifying pulse.

Move your left hand to the abdomen and the right hand to the right thigh. Hold and wait for the unifying pulse.

Place a hand on each foot and wait for the unifying pulse.

Hold each Fire toe and wait for the unifying pulse. [See chart on page 202.]

Repeat moves going up the left side of the body.

Move your left hand to right thigh and right hand over the abdomen. Hold and wait for the unifying pulse.

Place the left hand to abdomen and right hand over the forehead. Hold and wait for the unifying pulse.

Return to the top of the body and repeat the head cradle.

SPECIFIC MODALITY

Chi Nei Tsang is a detoxifying system that consists of systematically massaging points of the digestive tract to relieve stagnation and improve elimination.

Fire energy is what it takes for the digestive system to work properly.

TAROT & BODYWORK, PRACTICE & FOODS

Water Chakra/Suit

SUBTLE MOVES

With the client lying on the stomach, go down the right side of the body, place your left hand on the left shoulder blade (the back side of the chest) and the right hand around the back side of the pelvis. Hold and wait for the unifying pulse.

Move your left hand to the backside of the pelvis and the right hand to the bottom of the right foot. Hold and wait for the unifying pulse.

Place a hand on each foot. Hold and wait for the unifying pulse.

Hold each Water toe and wait for the unifying pulse. [See chart on page 202.]

Repeat moves going up the left side of the body.

Move left hand to right foot.

Place the left hand to back of the pelvis and right hand to the back side of the chest.

End with a slow rocking motion over the entire back.

SPECIFIC MODALITY

Reflexology applies pressure to special points that relate to zones and body reflexes on the feet, hands, and even ears. This can cause further relaxation of the nervous system, increased circulation, and stimulate the digestive tract. The feet are associated with both the Water Element and Chakra.

The first time I had a reflexology session, I thought I had died and gone to heaven. I walked from the class in Chelsea to my loft in Tribeca on the streets of NYC feeling as if my feet were cushions. Since the feet reflect your entire body, massaging them can relax just about everything.

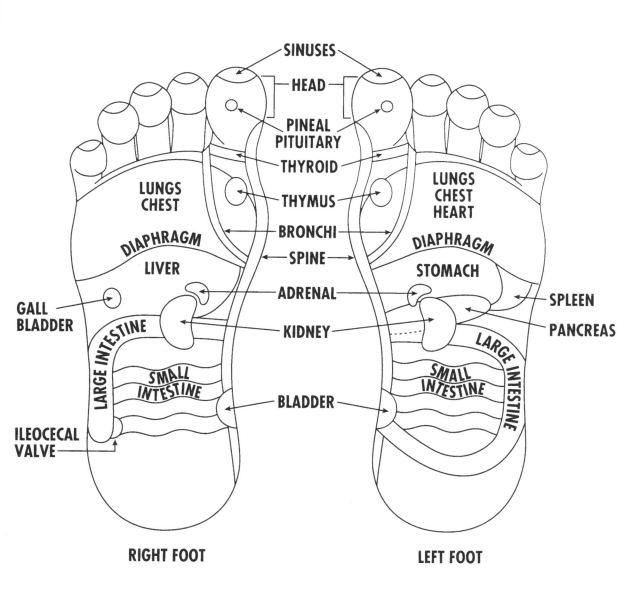

RIGHT FOOT   **LEFT FOOT**

TAROT & BODYWORK, PRACTICE & FOODS

 Earth Chakra/Suit

SUBTLE MOVES

With the client lying on the back, start with a head cradle.

Going down the right side of the body, place your left hand under the neck and the right hand over the lower abdomen (colon). Hold and wait for the unifying pulse.

Place your left hand over the lower abdomen and right hand over the knee. Hold and wait for the unifying pulse.

Move to the feet. Hold and wait for the unifying pulse.

Touch the Earth toes with each hand. Hold and wait for the unifying pulse. [See chart on page 202.]

Repeat moves going up the left side of the body.

Move your left hand to the right knee and your right hand to over the abdomen. Hold and wait for the unifying pulse.

Now, place your left hand over the abdomen and right hand under the neck. Hold and wait for the unifying pulse.

Return to the top of the body and repeat the head cradle.

SPECIFIC MODALITY

Massage Therapy works with manipulating muscles, soft tissues, and joints. Massage is most often done with oils or lotions directly applied to the skin. Benefits include increased blood flow, mental and physical relaxation, decreased stress, diminished muscle tension, and improved range of motion.

Massage Therapy is the most tactile and versatile of bodywork. It is also the most popular and ranges from deep tissue to lymph drainage, sports and pregnancy massage.

Shortly after Bob's wife died, he was referred to me. He has had many accidents and surgeries, which have resulted in many physical ailments. At eighty-five, his large frame cannot keep up with his active mind. My intention in working with Bob is not only to relieve his aches and pains, but also to encourage his awareness of his limitations and to increase his physical flexibility.

With Bob, I combine deep massage and Polarity point work with light energetic touch to encourage circulation.

The Tarot and Body-Based Practices

Body-based practices can enhance and integrate the lessons offered in each card. These practices are taken from the Polarity Wellness Tarot User's Guide.[1]

To decide what practice from which card to do, see what jumps out. Use a crystal pendulum over the cards. Use a practice from an element/Chakra/suit that does not appear in your reading.

MAJOR ARCANA – MEDITATION RITUALS

Making daily practices a ritual sets the intention. These practices reflect in a creative way what each card has to offer in simple conscious terms.

MINOR ARCANA – YOGA-LIKE EXERCISES

Enhances the benefits of any kind of physical movement. Choices of these exercises directly correspond to the somatic attributions of Polarity Wellness Tarot. These exercises are inspired by Polarity Therapy teachers.

COURT CARDS – ART RITUALS

Every element has an art form.

This is where we (Stephanie Swafford and I) had the most fun. In other words, we developed our own rituals. We took the art form and considered the type of court person and its Sub-Element that would to be the most appropriate action to take.[2]

TAROT & BODYWORK, PRACTICE & FOODS

ART FORMS

Air	dance
Fire	visual arts
Water	cooking
Earth	sculpture and aroma therapy

MAJOR ARCANA PRACTICES

0 Fool (no element) ···

Practice: Jump and skip as if you were a child, play hide and seek, or twirl in a circle.

ETHER CARDS

I The Magician ···

Practice: Inhale through both nostrils, filling your lungs and belly. Exhale through your mouth, with awareness of air passing through your entire torso, arms, and legs. Set your mind to do the task at hand.

II High Priestess ···

Practice: Sit comfortably with your feet on the ground. Become aware of the love in your heart and allow that to expand outward to all.

III The Empress ···

Practice: Breathe into your heart. Feel love for Mother Nature.

IV The Emperor ···

Practice: Breathe into your mid-torso. Have gratitude. Feel reverence.

V Hierophant ··

Practice: Give thanks to all the teachers that you've had. Appreciate the role that tradition and structure have played in your life. Remember everything is only a lesson.

VI Lovers ···

Practice: Open your heart to another person, an aspect of yourself, or to the world. Hear your own heartbeat. Feel that love as a reflection of yourself.

VII The Chariot

Practice: Enjoy your accomplishments and conquests. Become aware that you have the ability to take the reins in your own hands and move forward.

THIRD EYE CARDS

VIII Strength

Practice: Stand tall, expand your chest, feel your feet being grounded. Feel this strength emanating from the middle of your torso.

IX The Hermit

Practice: Draw attention inward. Know that only within yourself will you find your deeper truths.

X Wheel of Fortune

Practice: Be aware of powerful changes with perseverance. Trust that energy always changes.

XI Justice

Practice: Allow yourself to ponder fairness. Consider what this involves.

XII Hanged Man

Practice: Look at things from a different perspective. Stand on your head. Let the blood rush away from your feet.

XIII Death

Practice: Take a shower using a body scrub of salt.

XIV Temperance

Practice: Balance each foot on separate stones or surfaces. Calm any sensations in your body. Let your mind and Spirit become aware of the space around you.

CROWN CARDS

XV The Devil

Practice: Be mischievous.

XVI Tower

Practice: Recognize that after things fall apart, a resurrection happens. Clean your home or workspace with this intention.

TAROT & BODYWORK, PRACTICE & FOODS

XVII The Star ···
Practice: Close your eyes. Lift your head up high. Allow the glow of yourself to flow through you.

XVIII The Moon ···
Practice: Become aware of the phases of the moon and how you relate to them – waxing, waning, new, or full.

XIX The Sun ···
Practice: Go outside on a sunny day. Feel the warmth and power of the sun filling your body with pure joy.

XX Judgment ···
Practice: Be wide-awake with presence. Become aware of the cosmic forces at hand.

XXI The World
···
Practice: Dance wherever you are – to music or among the trees. Feel the joy of being alive in the beautiful abundant world.

Minor Arcana - Yoga-like Exercises and Court Cards - Art Rituals

AIR CARDS

Ace of Air ···
Practice: Clear your head. Stand tall. Shake your shoulders. Let your thoughts settle into clear intentions for the task at hand.

Two of Air ···
Practice: Moves torso energy. While standing, place your hands on either side of your rib cage. Breathe fully and move your torso from side to side.

Three of Air ···
Practice: Stretches back and releases tension. Stand with feet shoulder width apart. Slowly lean back with arms out stretched.

Four of Air ··

Practice: Mindful breathing. Place the hands on the back of your rib cage, fingers pointed towards your spine. With awareness, exaggerate breathing in and out.

Five of Air ··

Practice: Stimulates circulation. Lie on your stomach with forehead flat on the hands. Bend the knees and cross the feet at the ankles. Reverse and repeat.

Six of Air ··

Practice: Ankle rotations I. Lie on your back, reach legs up to the ceiling. Point your toes on one foot, leading with your big toe trace the letters of your name. Repeat with your other foot.

Seven of Air
··

Practice: Ankle rotations II. Sit and lift one foot off the ground at a time. Rotate the ankle counter clockwise, then clockwise.

Eight of Air ··

Practice: Releases tension in shoulders and arms. Stand up tall. Interlace fingers behind back, gently raise the arms and slowly bend forward.

Nine of Air ··

Practice: Releases negativity and shoulder tension. Stand up straight, place hands on shoulders or keep arms straight. Rotate arms in small to large circles in both directions.

Ten of Air ··

Practice: Loosens shoulder stress. Stand and slowly shrug shoulders up and down. Roll your head gently from side to side. Let it fall forward slowly. Inhale while turning to one side. Exhale while turning to the other side. Repeat.

King of Air ··

Practice: Dance to marching music, drums, or deep rhythms.

Queen of Air ··

Practice: Dance in free-form or with flowing scarves.

Knight of Air ··

Practice: Dance to club or hip-hop music.

Page of Air ··

Practice: Dance randomly like you did as a child.

TAROT & BODYWORK, PRACTICE & FOODS

Ace of Fire

Practice: Prepares you to take action. Stand with awareness. Place your hands on your mid-torso. Rub your tummy counter clockwise, then clockwise.

Two of Fire

Practice: Enhances movement and relaxes eyes. With eyes closed, look inward, move eyes up and down as if seeing the back of your head and around each ear. Look up to the top of your head then gently look down to your feet.

Three of Fire

Practice: Expands vision, deepens intuition. Take a look at something new. Let it sink in. Close your eyes. Recreate it in your mind's eye. Open your eyes and see how accurate you are.

Four of Fire

Practice: Calms, centers and rejuvenates. Sit cross-legged with your spine straight. Rest one hand on your forehead and one on your abdomen. Close your eyes and breath deeply. Repeat with reversed hand positions.

Five of Fire

Practice: Relaxes the back. Lie flat on your back with legs straight. Bend your knees, cradling them to the chest. Rock gently from side to side. Notice your back lengthening.

Six of Fire

Practice: Stretches calf muscles. Position the feet pointing straight ahead in a stride position. Bend both knees. Lift the back heel, and then slowly lower it. Repeat on the other side.

Seven of Fire

Practice: Enhances digestion. Stand, kneel or sit on heels. Exhale and bend forward while pressing the fingers on lower ribs.

Eight of Fire

Practice: Creates action. Bend your knees and slightly pitch forward at the hips. With your palms on the top of your thighs, sweep your palms downward towards your knees. Make a loud fiery "RAM" sound.

Nine of Fire ··

Practice: Releases pent up emotion, facilitates a "can do" attitude. Stand with legs apart. Clasp hands overhead. Bend forward and swing the arms through the legs making a "HA" sound.

Ten of Fire ···

Practice: Integrates and focuses. Swing the arms out to the left side. Reach out with the right foot. Repeat on other side. Let the limbs be relaxed like a pendulum.

King of Fire ··

Practice: Carve wood or design computer art.

Queen of Fire ··

Practice: Paint with watercolors, draw with ink or write calligraphy.

Knight of Fire ···

Practice: Draw with chalk or create a mural.

Page of Fire ··

Practice: Finger paint or color with crayons.

WATER CARDS

Ace of Water ···

Practice: Opens heart. Stand tall. Put your hands over your heart. Feel it beating. Let the pulse reconnect you to your deep emotions.

Two of Water ··

Practice: Awakens potential. Take a wide stance with hands on hips. Step forward onto right foot into a gentle lunge. Turn torso to the right and hold. Step back. Repeat on left side.

Three of Water ··

Practice: Strengthens muscles around the heart. Stand and place hands on shoulders. Move arms in so that the elbows touch each other, then move them back out. Repeat several times.

Four of Water ···

Practice: Increases sense of wellbeing. Place one hand on your chest or navel. Place the first two fingers of the other hand behind your ear. Hold. Reverse and repeat.

TAROT & BODYWORK, PRACTICE & FOODS

Five of Water ···
Practice: Relieves compression on the spine. Take a wide stance. With arms straight, slide hands down to the mid thighs, while you are bending your knees. Turn head and shoulders to one side, feeling the twist in the torso. Repeat on other side.

Six of Water ···
Practice: Relieves leg cramps. Sit on the floor with your legs extended in front of you. Roll legs back and forth from the hip joint in a flowing movement similar to windshield wipers.

Seven of Water ···
Practice: Releases spinal and pelvic muscles. Lay on your back. Cradle your knees as you rotate them counter clock-wise. Repeat in a clockwise motion.

Eight of Water ···
Practice: Strengthens foot muscles. Pick up several marbles, or small rocks, with your toes. Drop them into a bowl.

Nine of Water ···
Practice: Improves balance and focus. Walk an imaginary line, one foot in front of the other. Repeat walking backwards.

Ten of Water ··
Practice: Stimulates nerve endings in feet. Massage feet slowly. Press into any tender points.

King of Water ···
Practice: Bake or grill food.

Queen of Water ···
Practice: Cook soup or make a fruit salad.

Knight of Water ···
Practice: Make a cup of sweet hot tea or stir fry vegetables.

Page of Water ···
Practice: Bake cookies or make applesauce.

EARTH CARDS

Ace of Earth ··
Practice: Creates structure for intention. Stand tall. Allow your feet to make contact with the earth. Feel every point of both feet evenly balanced on the ground. Prepare to step forward.

Two of Earth

Practice: Encourages full body connection. Stand tall, with feet shoulder width apart. Stretch hands towards the ceiling. Shrug your shoulders up towards your ears and then down. Elongate your neck.

Three of Earth

Practice: Increases flexibility. Stand with your legs together. Place your hands just above your slightly bent knees. Make circles with the knees to the left and then to the right.

Four of Earth

Practice: Opens pelvis. Bend your knees and come down into a low squat position. Keep heels as flat as possible on floor. Relax and stretch from your neck to the base of your spine. Allow your arms to cradle your knees.

Five of Earth

Practice: Releases held tension. Stand with feet shoulder width apart. Slowly lean back with arms outstretched.

Six of Earth

Practice: Relaxes shoulders. Slowly turn the head to look over and behind you. Repeat on other side.

Seven of Earth

Practice: Releases neck tension. Roll your neck carefully in full circles. Breathe into any tight spots.

Eight of Earth

Practice: Stretches spine and back muscles. Kneel on the floor with your arms stretched out in front of you. Rest your forehead on the floor. Let your neck and head relax. Stretch your back away from your hips.

Nine of Earth

Practice: Stimulates digestion. Lie down on your back with your knees bent. Gently rub tummy in a counter clock-wise motion around your navel. Reverse clockwise.

Ten of Earth

Practice: Open pelvis again. Stand with legs shoulder with apart. Slowly squat down, getting your feet as flat on the ground as possible. With your fingers, press your outer calves.

King of Earth

Practice: Work with clay. Walk in wet sand or mud.

TAROT & BODYWORK, PRACTICE & FOODS

Queen of Earth ···

Practice: Use sweet or calming scents on pulse points. Create with papier maché.

Knight of Earth ···

Practice: Burn sage. Build a sand castle.

Page of Earth ···

Practice: Create with Play Doh™. Make mud pies.

All "Practices" are from PWT User's guide

The Body, the Tarot, and Foods

Food is an integral part of life and the most direct and tangible way to change our physiology and our frame of mind. In my experience, many people would rather die than change their diets. Others will try just about any diet.

Following an Ayurveda diet is one of most sophisticated and oldest ways to bring the body back into balance. Ayurveda offers a brilliant and complex way to tailor what foods and spices are best for an individual at a given time, along with other lifestyle practices, to obtain optimum health. A trained Ayurvedic practitioner consultation is necessary to determine what course of action to take.

In the 1940s to the 1950s, Randolph Stone simplified Ayurveda's view of food as a self-help tool to change the energy in the body. Although Stone's Health Building does not entirely do Ayurveda justice, I believe it opened a door for Westerners to look at how food affects us on an energetic level.

The concept is that foods that grow farther away from the earth were less dense. This mirrors the Chakras, which also get less dense as they move up the spine. If an element was missing, it could easily be obtained by a food in a particular category.

What I've done here is to take Stone's Health Building concepts a step further. I've interpreted elemental food growing heights to the Minor Arcana Chakra/Suits. Tarot may be used as an indication of what to include in our diets. I've matched the individual cards with the quality of that particular food that seemed most appropriate. Food references only appear in the Minor Arcana interpretations of the suit cards.

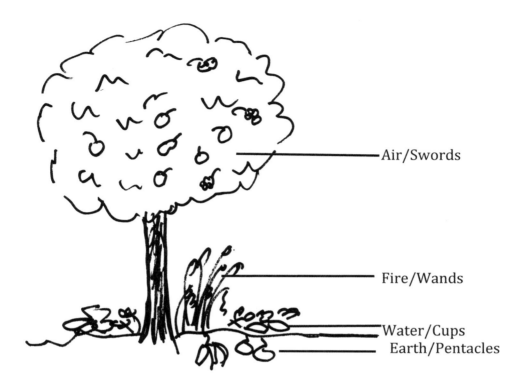

Air/Swords

Fire/Wands

Water/Cups
Earth/Pentacles

Starting with foods grown under the ground, there are the root vegetables. These are attributed to the Pentacle/Earth Chakra/Suit.

From the ground up to two feet are leafy green vegetables and melons. These relate to the Cups/Water Chakra/Suit.

Next are grains that grow to two to six feet above the ground. They relate to the Wands/ Fire Chakra/Suit.

Then there are fruits, nuts, and seeds that grow six feet or more. They are associated with the Swords/Air Chakra/Suit.

The day of my graduation ceremony from my first level of Polarity Therapy training, I was so excited I could hardly focus. I had a lot to accomplish, including making a potluck dish for the reception. I was having a hard time getting anything done. I then remembered my Health Building training. I baked a potato and ate it. I then became grounded and focused. In hindsight, I would have invoked a few Tarot cards, such as the nine or ten Earth/Pentacles, or perhaps done an Earth meditation.

TAROT & BODYWORK, PRACTICE & FOODS

This list is by no means precise. For serious conditions consult a physician before working with any new diet. Mix and match; follow your body reactions and pull a few cards to monitor the effects.

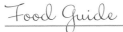

SWORDS/AIR CHAKRA/SUIT

Ace	Cherries
Two	Oranges
Three	Peaches
Four	Pears
Five	Lemons
Six	Apples
Seven	Walnuts
Eight	Pecans
Nine	Plums
Ten	Bananas

WANDS/FIRE CHAKRA/SUIT

Ace	Wheat
Two	Pinto Beans
Three	Black Beans
Four	Millet
Five	Rice
Six	Chickpeas
Seven	Barley
Eight	Oats
Nine	Corn
Ten	Quinoa

CUPS/WATER CHAKRA/SUIT

Ace	Lettuces
Two	Watermelon
Three	Cantaloupe
Four	Kale
Five	Chard
Six	Collard Greens
Seven	Cucumbers
Eight	Green Beans
Nine	Berries
Ten	Honeydew

PENTACLE/EARTH CHAKRA/SUIT

Ace	Russet Potatoes
Two	Daikon
Three	Radishes
Four	Parsnips
Five	Onions
Six	Yams
Seven	Turnips
Eight	Beets
Nine	Sweet Potatoes
Ten	Carrots

HOME REMEDIES FOR CHAKRA BALANCING

CHAPTER 13

The most empowering healing we can perform is the healing we do for ourselves. Ultimately, body workers, therapists, and healers are mere channels or guides. Eventually, we are responsible for taking charge of our own wellbeing.

Here are some Chakra/Element/Suit home remedies you can do for yourself. Many are based on Ayurvedic practices that I have learned over the years. Ayurveda balances the life energy in the body back to its original, optimum state – not only by food, but also by five major purification and cleansing procedures known as *Panchakarma*, some of which are included below.

All home remedies are organized according to how they correspond to the individual Elements/Chakras.

Crown Balance Home Remedy

SHIRODHORA

This procedure, derived from Ayurveda, involves "the dripping of oil like a thread." Shirodhora calms the mind and the central nervous system. While lying down, face-up, a steady stream of warm oil is poured onto the area of your forehead avoiding the eyes from a vessel suspended above the head. The oil then slowly drips down through the hair and is then caught in second vessel.

While my friend George was studying Ayurveda, he decided to practice Shirodora treatments on me. I received treatments for two consecutive days. Not only was I extremely calm, my brain seemed to have been "oiled" and was functioning at optimum levels. The following day, I had the ability to intuitively access driving directions in a city I had never visited.

BEDTIME OIL HEAD MASSAGE

Before going to sleep, place some coconut oil in the palm of your hand. Add a few drops of your favorite essential oil.

Rub until the oil liquefies, then rub into your scalp with your fingers.

Repeat until your entire scalp is covered in oil.

Comb the oil through your hair. Wear a scarf or hat to bed.

In the morning, wash your hair several times.

Third Eye Balance Home Remedy

NASYA

Nasya, also a Panchakarma procedure, cleanses and rejuvenates the tissues in the head and neck. Naysa is the nostril administration of medicated oils. In a professional setting, more oil would be administered, possibly a medicated oil with specifically tailored herbs for your balance.

Lie face up with your head tilted back slightly.

Place 3–5 drops of warmed sesame oil in each nostril.

Massage in and around your nostrils.

Other Balance Home Remedy

Tongue Cleaning involves gently scraping away residual coating on the tongue before brushing your teeth. This process comprises an early stage of cleansing the digestive tract. Take an Ayurvedic oral health tongue scraper, and gently scrape down your tongue several times each morning. The color of the tongue and the coating reflects how your digestive system is functioning.

Horseshoe-shaped tongue scrapers may be purchased at Indian food markets or through online Ayurvedic stores. A metal spoon may also be used.

TAROT & BODYWORK, PRACTICE & FOODS

BIOSONIC TUNING FORKS™

A favorite home remedy of mine for balancing any of the Chakras, especially the Ether Chakra (because it relates to sound) is the practice of balancing our vestibular nervous system with the use of pure-note tuning forks.

Musician John Beaulieu, ND, PhD, discovered hearing his nervous system in a completely soundproof chamber. From this he developed Biosonic Repatterning™ to help tone and bring the body back into resonance.

The Solar Harmonic Spectrum[1], a set of eight forks, creates different intervals to activate different elemental qualities that are easily translated to Chakras. The forks are gently tapped and held near the ears or over the entire body. The effects include relaxation, physical awareness, and refinement of your sonic abilities.

Air Balance Home Remedies

ABHYANGA

Abhyanga detoxifies the body by lubricating the skin with generous amounts of oil. The skin is associated with the Air Element and the Heart Chakra, and is our largest organ. A daily self-administered Abhyanga oil massage increases circulation, decreases dryness, and calms the nervous system. If our nerves are calm, our thoughts calm down, which in turn soothes the heart.

Abhyanga oil massage is best done right before taking a shower. I suggest using sesame seed oil if your skin is dry or coconut oil for less dryer skin.

> *Warm the oil if possible by placing a smaller plastic container of the oil in warm water.*
>
> *Massage generous amounts of oil in long strokes up all of your muscles towards your heart. Massage oil in circular movements into the joints.*
>
> *Allow five to twenty minutes for the oil to penetrate before stepping into a shower.*

Additional Tips
- Use an organic cold press oil whenever possible.
- Do not use toasted sesame seed oil (the kind generally used for Asian cooking).

- Avoid taking your oil directly from the glass jar you bought it in.
- Be sure the bathroom is kept warm.
- Coconut oil is recommended for skin rashes and irritations, to be applied after any shower.
- Do not administer this procedure during menses or an illness.

Fire Balance Home Remedies

STOMACH RUB

This is a self-administered version of a Chi Nei Tsang practice.

Lay on your back with your knees bent and your feet on the floor.

Put a pillow under your knees or lean your knees against each other.

With loose or open pants, start massaging around your belly button in a clockwise motion.

Continue this motion, slowly and gently, going deeper. If a spot is sore, stay there for a few minutes and massage a little deeper, bringing circulation to that particular area until there's a loosening of tension.

As you circle around, move out and away from your belly button.

Recipe to aid in producing digestive Fire
MUNG DAL KITCHARI

An adapted recipe from Dr. Lad's Ayurvedic recipe book. Kitchari is a staple food in an Ayurvedic diet.

1 cup basmati rice
1/2 cup yellow split mung dal
3 tablespoons ghee (clarified butter)
1 teaspoon black mustard seeds
1 teaspoon cumin
2 pinches asafetida
1/2 teaspoon turmeric
1/2 teaspoon salt
4 cups water

TAROT & BODYWORK, PRACTICE & FOODS

Wash rice and dal well. You may soak the dal for a few hours before cooking.
Cook rice and dal in water. Add more water if necessary.

In a saucepan over medium heat, melt the ghee and add mustard seeds and asafetida (hing) first. Stir until mustard seeds pop. Then add the other spices, leaving the turmeric for last. Add ghee mixture to rice and dal.

Variations
- Add and subtract other spices in various proportions; garam marsala, cinnamon, cardamom, coriander, curry leaves etc.
- Use just two spices such as asafoetida and garam marsala.
- Substitute red lentils or whole green dal beans for yellow dal.
- Cook rice and dal with spices and add ghee to serving bowls.
- Cook kitchari with a vegetable such as carrots or zucchini.
- Add separately cooked vegetables to kitchari

Ghee: Ayurvedic cooking uses ghee as its source of oil, to aid in digestion by lubricating the digestive system. Ghee is also known as clarified butter.

Heat 1 pound of organic sweet, unsalted butter in a saucepan over low heat until it separates from the milk solids (white foam).

Either scoop out foam as it rises to top or allow it to form a crust on the bottom of the saucepan.

When your ghee smells like popcorn and turns a darker yellow remove from heat.

After twenty minutes, strain with a fine mesh strainer into a sterilized jar. You may keep your ghee on the counter top. Do not place a utensil with any other foods or liquids (especially water) into your ghee jar.

Water Balance Home Remedy

Create this bath as a ritual.

Fill a tub with hot water and a full cup of mineral salts.

Add a few drops of the oil of your choice; Lavender, ylang-ylang, rose or geranium oil are some possible choices.

Burn candles or dim the lights, play music that brings up fond memories.

Soak in the tub for at least twenty minutes.

If you sense a cold or flu coming on (a water disorder), an alternative to getting sick would be to fill the tub up with water as hot as you can tolerate. Pour 16 oz. of apple cider vinegar into the water. Climb into the bath and make sure your entire body is immersed. Stay and sweat until the water begins to cool down.

Quickly, after drying off, dress in several layers of warm bed clothing and go straight to bed, making sure that you have plenty of extra blankets at hand. Do not even stop to make a cup of tea or put something away, because you will lose heat necessary to flush out your cold. You should sweat profusely during the night, and may even need to prepare a change of clothing for later in the night. Place this at the end of your bed so you can change swiftly, without becoming chilled.

Earth Balance Home Remedy

Walk barefoot in mud or wet sand.

Give yourself a clay mask.

Feel your feet on any surface.

Imagine the four corners of each foot equally balanced on the ground. Or imagine the balance as a triangle. If they do not feel balanced gently push down on the point that feels slightly off the ground.

SESAME SEED OIL FOOT RUB

(This may also be done for water balance since the feet are represented by the Water Element).

The feet are the most negative pole in the body, which means they are most receptive to remedies and healing.

It is best to use warm oil. Use an organic cold press oil whenever possible.

Do not use toasted sesame seed oil, the kind generally used for Asian cooking.

Rub sesame seed oil into your feet.

Have a reflexology chart handy to check reflex points of the body.

Balance and ground all the elements by gently pinching, rubbing or massaging the toes and toe pads.

TAROT & BODYWORK, PRACTICE & FOODS

Tarot Elements and Toe Correlations:

Large Toe: Major Arcana
Pointer Toe: Air
Middle Toe: Fire
Ring Toe: Water
Pinkie toe: Earth

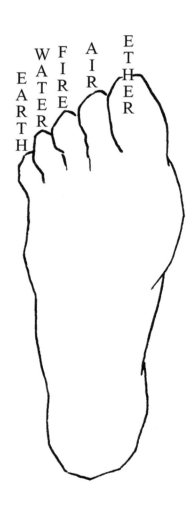

Full List of Suit Self-Soothers for Chakra Calming and Toning

(Individually listed under each Chakra)

CROWN CHAKRA/MA XV–XXI SUIT SELF-SOOTHER

Keep one end of the hand lightly on the top of your head and over your forehead with or without actually touching. Invoke clarity and connection to the universe. After a few minutes, when you can feel the pulses resonate, move both hands to the top of the head.

THIRD EYE CHAKRA/ MA VIII–XIV SUIT SELF-SOOTHER

Rub both hands together until you feel heat. Then, cupping your hands slightly, place them over your forehead and eyes. Move your hands very slowly in a circle. Feel the warmth from your hands. Imagine light energy coming from your hands. Ask for clarity of purpose.

ETHER CHAKRA/MAA I–VI SUIT SELF-SOOTHER

Keep your hands soft and relaxed. The touch is light. Interlace your fingers and cradle the back of you head. Your thumbs should rest by the side of the neck. Send an intention of allowing more space and understanding of archetypical experiences.

AIR CHAKRA /SUIT SELF-SOOTHER

Keep your hands soft and relaxed. The touch is light. Place one hand on the back or your neck and one hand on your heart, the Air Chakra. Gently rub your heart. Breathe and feel the quality of your breath. Calm any scattered thoughts or quick movements with a gentle cool lightness.

FIRE CHAKRA/SUIT SELF-SOOTHER

Place both hands over the abdomen, palms facing inward. Your thumbs and index fingers are touching. The touch is light. Imagine a mirror around your solar plexus. Imagine sending spontaneity and passion throughout your body.

TAROT & BODYWORK, PRACTICE & FOODS

WATER CHAKRA/SUIT SELF-SOOTHER

Keep your hands soft and relaxed. Place one hand over your forehead and one on your lower abdomen. With nurturing feelings send a warm flowing energy throughout your body.

EARTH CHAKRA/SUIT SELF-SOOTHER

Keep your hands soft yet solid. Place one hand on the back of the neck, and one on your back at the base of your spine. Feel your feet solidly on the ground. Project a feeling of earthy security and safety.

Complete Chart of Connecting Systems

	ETHER	AIR	FIRE	WATER	EARTH
TAROT	Major Arcana	Swords	Wands	Cups	Pentacles
CHAKRA	Throat	Heart	Solar plexus	Sexual	Root
ASTROLOGY	All signs	Gemini, Libra, Aquarius	Aries, Leo, Sagittarius	Cancer, Scorpio, Pisces	Taurus, Virgo, Capricorn
SOUND	Ham	Yam	Ram	Vam	Lam
GEMSTONE	moonstone	emerald	coral	pearl	ruby
ART	music	dance	visual arts	cooking	sculpture and aromatherapy
EMOTIONS	joy, grief, emptiness	compassion, greed, charity, desire	enthusiasm, excitement, anger, resentment	letting go, attachment	courage, fear, secure/insecure
PHYSICAL BODY	hear	shoulders, kidneys, ankles, chest and lungs, nervous system	forehead, solar plexus, thighs, digestive system, liver etc.	chest, generative organs, feet, lymphatic system	neck, colon, knees, bones, blood
SENSE	all joints	touch	see	taste	smell
TISSUE QUALITY	elongation	movement, speed, nerve reflexes	shaking, heat	smooth, flowing	strength, muscle tone, contracting
VOICE QUALITY	open, dense, silence	fast, jumpy, breathy, scattered	loud, sharp, staccato	rhythmic, smooth, flowing	slow, steady, deep

ENDNOTES

Introduction

1. For more information and support groups on near death experiences, go to the International Association for Near Death Studies IANDS.

Glossary

1. Renée, Bornstein, Psychological Astrologer and Director of Café Aquarius Astrology Center, Emeryville, CA.

Chapter I

1. Arrien, Angeles. *The Tarot Handbook. Challenge cards*. (Sonoma, CA: Tarcher Putnam 1987), pg. 213.

Chapter II

1. Most notable in the King James Version of the Bible: The Book of Genesis, The beginning 1:1–2 [every version is slightly different].

2. German-born theoretical physicist Albert Einstein (1879–1955) established the Theory of Relativity in 1916.

3. Arewa, pg.19.

Chapter III

1. Tassajara Zen Mountain Center is part of the San Francisco Zen Center.

2. Much of what I've learned about Tara has been from conversations over the years with Tara practitioner Jenny Holland.

3. I first learned this technique from Rev. Dr. Hedy Milicevic (1922–), a spiritual doctor I studied with for several years in NYC.

Chapter VI

1. PBS Nova special on Building Pharaoh's Chariot aired 02/06/13.

2. Martel.

3. Jenny.

Chapter VII

1. From lecture Gregg Braden, Salt Lake City, UT 2006.

2. HeartMath performs research on linking emotion, heart function, and cognitive performance and bringing them into balance.

3. Sam Beckett, Irish playwright quote (1906–1989).

4. Roddenberry, Gene. Star Trek: The Next Generation. (TV series, 1987–1993).

Chapter XIII

1. Biosonic Enterprises – John Beaulieu.

Arewa, Caroline Shola. *Opening to Spirit.* (London, UK: HarperCollins, 1998).

Arrien, Angeles. *The Tarot Handbook.* (Sonoma, CA: Tarcher Putnam 1987).

Aurobindo, Sri. Compiled by A.S. Dalal. *The Psychic Being, Soul: Nature, Mission and Evolution.* (Wilmot WI, Lotus Light Publications. 1990).

Bartlett, Sarah. *The Tarot Bible.* (New York: Sterling Publishing, 2006).

Beaulieu, Dr. John. *Polarity Therapy Workbook.* (New York, NY: Biosonic Enterprises, Ltd, 1994).

Beaulieu, Dr. John. *Human Tuning.* (High Falls, NY: Biosonic Enterprises, 2010).

Braden, Gregg. *The Divine Matrix: Bridging Time, Space, Mircles and Belief.* (USA, Hay House 2007).

Brown, Edward Espe. *Tassajara Cooking.* (Boston, MA: Shambhala Publications, 1985).

Chia, Mantak and Maneewan. *Chi Nei Tsang, Internal Organ Massage.* (Huntington, NY: Healing Tao Books, 1990).

Chia, Mantak and Maneewan. *Cultivating Female Sexual Energy.* (Huntington, NY: Healing Tao Books, 1986).

Chitty, John and Mary Louise Muller. *Easy Exercises for Health and Vitality.* (Boulder, CO, Polarity Press, 1992).

Crowley, Aleister. *The Book of Thoth: A Short Essay on the Tarot of the Egyptians.* (York Beach, ME: Samuel Weiser, Republished 1969).

Das, Bhagavan. *It's Here Now (Are You?).* (New York, NY: Broadway Books, 1967).

Dickens, Charles. *A Christmas Carol.* (ReadaClassic.com 2010).

Dossey, Larry. *Prayer is Good Medicine: How to Reap the Benefits of Prayer.* (San Francisco, CA, HarperSanFrancisco 1996).

Frawley, David. *Yoga and Ayurveda.* (Twin Lakes, WI: Lotus Press, 1999).

Einstein, Albert. *Realativity the Special and General Theory.* (Penguin Classics Worldwide 2006, first published 1916).

Greer, Mary. *Tarot for Yourself.* (Franklin Lakes, NJ, New Page Books 2002).

Gyatso, Geshe Kelsang. *Universal Compassion.* (London, UK: Tharpa Publications 1997).

Hall, Judy. *The Crystal Bible 2,* (Cincinnati, OH: Walking Stick Press, 2009).

Hill, Deborah Ardell. *Spiritual Reflexology.* (Sacramento, CA: DAH Enterprises. 1999).

Jenny, Hans. *Cymatics: The Structure and Dymanics of Waves and Vibrations.* (Basel, Switzerland: Basilius Presse, 1974).

Joshi, Sunil V. *Ayurveda and Panchkarma. The Science of Healing and Rejuvenation.* (Twin Lakes, WI: Lotus Press, 1997).

Judith, Anodea. *Eastern Body Western Mind, Psychology and the Chakra System.* (Berkeley CA: Celestial Arts, 1996).

Judith, Anodea. *Wheels of Life: A User's Guide to the Chakra System.* (Woodbury, MN: Llewellyn Worldwide, 1988).

Kapit, Wynn and Lawrence M. Elson Lawrence. *The Anatomy Coloring Book: Second Edition.* (New York, NY: Harper Collins, 1993).

Katz, Marcus. *Tarosophy® Fast Track Kabbalah.* (Tarot Professionals, England, GB 2010).

King James Bible: The Beginning (Genesis 1:1–2) (Thomas Nelson; New edition July 5, 2005).

Lad, Vasant. *Ayurveda, The Science of Life: A Practical Guide.* (Twin Lakes, WI: Lotus Press, 1984).

Lad, Vasant. *The Complete Book of Ayurvedic Home Remedies.* (New York, NY: Crown Publishing, 1998).

Martel, Yann. *Life of Pi.* (Random House, Canada: Harcourt Press, 2001).

Maslow, Abraham. *Religions, Values and Peak-Experiences.* (New York: Penguin Books, 1976).

Morningstar, Amedea. *The Ayurvedic Guide to Polarity Therapy.* (Twin Lakes, WI: Lotus Press, 2001).

Pollack, Rachel. *Tarot Wisdom.* (Woodbury, MN: Llewellyn Worldwide, 2009).

Sills, Franklyn. *The Polarity Process: Energy as a Healing Art.* (Berkeley, CA: North Atlantic Books, 1989, 2002).

Sherab, Khenchen Palden and Khenpo Tswang Dongyal. *Tara's Enlightened Activity.* (Boston, MASnow Lion Publications, 2004).

Stone, Dr. Randolph. *Polarity Therapy, The Complete Collected Works Volumes 1 and 2.* (Sebastopol, CA: CRCS Publications, 1986 – original works 1954–1957).

Stone, Dr. Randolph. *Health Building.* (Sebastopol CA: CRCS, 1985).

Joshi, Sunil V. Ayurveda and Panchkarma, *The Science of Healing and Rejuvenation.* (Twin Lakes, WI: Lotus Press, 1997).

BIBLIOGRAPHY

Thonduo Rinpoche, Tulku. *Boundless Healing: Meditation Exercises to Enlighten the Mind and Heal the Body.* (Boston, MA: Shambhala Publications, 2000).

Trungpa, Chogyam. *Cutting Through Spiritual Materialism*. (Boston, MA: Shambhala Publications 1973).

Upledger, John E. DO, FAAO and Vredevoogd MFA. *Craniosacral Therapy*. (Seattle WA: Eastland Press, 1983).

Vitruvius, *De Architectura libri X*, ed. F. Granger, London, 1962.

Wang, Robert. *The Qabalistic Tarot: A Textbook of Mystical Philosophy.* (York Beach, ME: Samuel Weiser, 1983).

Williams, Duncan Ryuken. *The Other Side of Zen*. (Princeton NJ: Princeton University Press, 2005).

Web References

http://www.brainyquote.com/quotes/quotes/s/samuelbeck121335.html

http://www.forthebodyandspirit.com/Bodywork_.html

https://www.goodreads.com/book/show/15852.Relativity

http://healing.about.com/od/gemstonesaz/

http://www.heartmath.com/

www.magick-crystal.com/

http://www.newdimensions.org/program-archive/the-power-of-prayer-with-larry-dossey-m-d

http://www.rosenmethod.com/index.html

http://www.sfzc.org/tassajara/

http://www.soularenergy.com/gemstones.html

http://www.tarothistory.com/index.html

http://en.wikipedia.org/wiki/Bodywork_%28alternative_medicine%29